TWEED YARN KNITTING

OVER 50 SUMPTUOUS WOOLEN PROJECTS

Trafalgar Square
North Pomfret, Vermont

First published in the United States of America
in 2016 by
Trafalgar Square Books
North Pomfret, Vermont 05053

Originally published in German as *Landlust Handarbeiten mit Tweedgarn*.

Copyright © 2014 Landwirtschaftsverlag GmbH, 48165 Münster, Germany (www.lv-buch.de)
English translation © 2016 Trafalgar Square Books, published by arrangement with Claudia
Böhme Rights & Literary Agency, Hannover, Germany (www.agency-boehme.com)

ISBN: 978-1-57076-766-1

Library of Congress Control Number: 2015960383

Concept Editors: Uta Böning, Ute Frieling-Huchzermeyer
Project Designers: Eva Varpio (34), Persis Klassen (6), Annette Rubertus (5),
Uta Böning (3), Béatrice Simon/lillicroche (2), Sarah Kate Spillane (1)
Editor: Uta Böning
Layout: Heike Gütting
Image Processing: Tanja Stegemann
Technical Editing: Eva Varpio, Martina Zeller, Beate Hauling
Drawings: Frank Hegemann, Eva Varpio, Béatrice Simon/lillicroche, Martina Zeller
Photos: Heinz Duttmann, Persis Klassen (22), Christian Malsch-von Stockhausen (14)
Translation: Donna Druchunas

Printed in China

10 9 8 7 6 5 4 3 2 1

Dear Reader,

A few years ago, we discovered a wonderful new tweed yarn from Ireland. Landlust Tweed is made in County Donegal at one of the last woolen mills remaining in the northwest of Ireland. The fleece is "dyed in the wool" in small batches and then spun with small slubs of color included to create the traditional look of classic tweed yarn.

Since then, Landlust has worked with designers to create many beautiful garments and accessories out of this unique wool yarn. In this book, we present 50 of our favorite designs from past issues, along with a couple brand new designs that haven't been published before. From hats and scarves, skirts and jumpers, to accessories for "at home or on the go," in these pages you'll find projects for knitters of all skill levels. Each of the 52 designs includes step-by-step instructions and beautiful photos so you can create your own wonderful projects. On the last few pages of the book you'll find a list of common abbreviations and other useful information.

Have fun knitting!

Your Landlust Editors

Hats, Scarves & Cuffs

Sweaters and Vests

Dresses and Skirts

At Home or On the Go

General Information

HATS, SCARVES & CUFFS

DROP STITCH
LADDER SCARF

1

RIB, BOBBLE, AND FRINGE SCARF

2

3

4

HEADBANDS

HAIR TIES

5

6

7 CABLED HATS

9

FUNKY POMPOM HAT

10
GREEN
WITH ENVY
CROCHETED
HAT

11/12 CROCHETED STRIPED TOQUES

13
WEATHER THE STORM SHAWL COLLAR

14
OUTRAGEOUSLY CUTE WRIST WARMERS

15
FABULOUS FRINGED WRIST WARMERS

16
COMFY CABLED
WRIST WARMERS

17

18

19

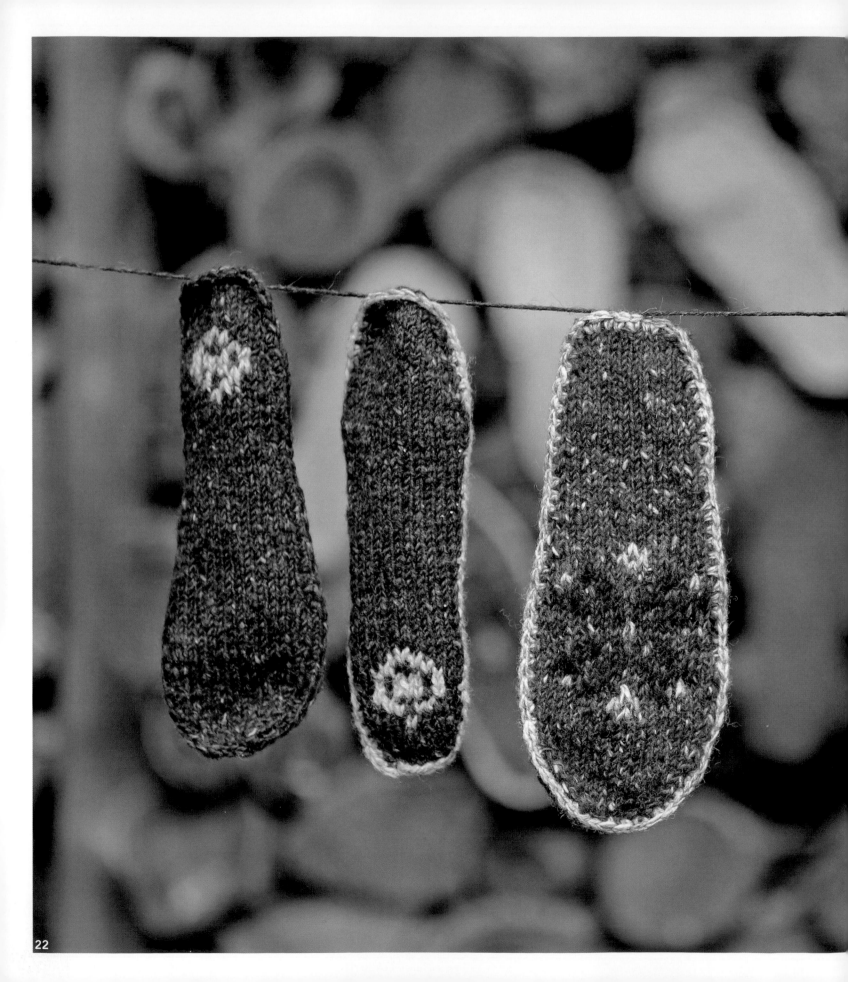

20
STEP IT UP
SHOE INSOLES

MATERIALS

Yarn:
CYCA #4 (worsted/afghan/
aran), Landlust Tweed or
equivalent (87 yd/80 m /
50 g)

Yarn Amounts:
#4989 Petrol Blue, 150 g

Knitting Needles:
U.S. size 10 / 6 mm

Crochet Hook:
U.S. J-10 / 6 mm

Notions:
2 strips of fabric such as
gauze (each approx. 4 x
71 in / 10 x 180 cm) long

Finished Measurements:
Approx. 71 in / 180 cm
long, depending on gauge
and felting

1 DROP STITCH LADDER SCARF

PATTERN

GAUGE
15 sts and 23 rows in St st = 4 x 4 in /
10 x 10 cm

PATTERN STITCH
Stockinette Stitch (St st): Knit RS
rows, purl WS rows.

INSTRUCTIONS
CO 22 sts and work in St st until
almost all of the yarn is used up. Make
sure your stitches are loose so the
fabric will felt easily. If necessary, use
larger needles.

BO, dropping stitches to form ladders
as follows: BO 3, drop 5 sts, use
crochet hook to chain 3 over gap
formed by dropped stitches; BO 6, drop
5 sts, ch 3.

Unravel the dropped stitches down to
the CO edge (the scarf will be stretchy
after dropping the stitches and should
easily stretch out to measure approx.
75-87 in / 190-220 cm long, depending on your gauge).

FINISHING

Weave the fabric strips through the
ladders of dropped stitches at regular
intervals of 4-8 rows, or at random
intervals if you prefer. Tie the ends of
the strips together so they don't come
out during felting in the washing
machine. (**Note:** The fabric strips are
used to make the felting process of the
dropped stitches irregular.)

Felt the scarf using hot water and the
normal cycle in the washing machine.
Rinse with hair conditioner if desired.

After felting the scarf, remove the
fabric strips, smooth the scarf so it lays
flat, and stretch it to the desired
length. Hang over the top of a door to
dry. If the scarf is still too fluffy, you
can put it in the dryer for 20 to 30
minutes. The scarf will shrink about 20
to 30 percent, and the finished size
will depend on your knitting gauge.

2 RIB, BOBBLE, AND FRINGE SCARF

PATTERN

GAUGE
18 sts and 23 rows in Knit Ribbing =
4 x 4 in / 10 x 10 cm

PATTERN STITCHES
Knit Ribbing: (K2, p2) across.
Crochet Patt: 1 sc, ch 1, make dc
bobble, ch 1. (See chart.)

INSTRUCTIONS
With knitting needles, CO 42 sts. Work
in Knit Ribbing until scarf measures
approx. 51 in / 130 cm. BO.
Work 8 in / 20 cm crochet border on
each end of the scarf as follows.

BORDER
Row 1: Work 27 sc into CO or BO edge
of scarf.
Row 2: Sc in first sc of prev row, * ch
1, make dc bobble in next st, ch 1, sc
in next sc; rep from * 5 more times. Ch
1, make dc bobble in next st, ch 1
(turning ch).
Rows 3-20: *Sc in the bobble from
prev row, ch 1, make dc bobble in next
st, ch 1; rep from * 6 times.
Fasten off.

FINISHING

Attach fringe to both ends of scarf.
Cut 4 pieces of yarn 19 in / 50 cm long
and fold them in half. Insert crochet
hook into edge of scarf, and pull fold
through. Pull ends of fringe through
folded piece and tug to tighten.

MATERIALS

Yarn:
CYCA #4 (worsted/afghan/
aran), Landlust Tweed or
equivalent (87 yd/80 m /
50 g)

Yarn Amounts:
#4754 Landlust Red or
#4582 Stone Gray, 300 g

Knitting Needles:
U.S. size 10 / 6 mm

Crochet Hook:
U.S. J-10 / 6 mm

Finished Measurements:
9½ in / 24 cm wide 67 in /
170 cm long, without
fringe

KEY

✕ single crochet = sc
◯ chain = ch
⑂ double crochet bobble = dc
bobble. Yo, insert hook in
next st, pull up a lp (3 lps on
hook). Yo, pull through 2 lps
(2 lps on hook). Yo insert in
same st, pull up a lp (4 lps
on hook). Yo, pull through 2
lps (3 lps on hook). Yo insert
in same st, pull up a lp (5 lps
on hook). Yo and pull through
2 lps (4 lps on hook). Yo pull
through all 4 lps.

CROCHET CHART

Row 3 · · · Row 2 · · · Row 1 · · · Repeat

3/4 HEADBANDS

MATERIALS

PETROL BLUE HEADBAND
Yarn:
CYCA #4 (worsted/afghan/
aran), Landlust Tweed
or equivalent
(87 yd/80 m / 50 g)

Yarn Amounts:
#4898 Petrol Blue, 50 g

Knitting Needles:
U.S. size 7 / 4.5 mm

Finished Measurements:
Approx. 21½ in / 55 cm
long, knit to desired
length to fit

**STRIPES AND TUCKS
HEADBAND**
Yarn:
CYCA #4 (worsted/
afghan/aran), Landlust
Tweed or equivalent
(87 yd/80 m / 50 g)

Yarn Amounts:
Total, approx. 50 g in 6
colors:
#4818 Plum
#4802 Rust
#4741 Dark Brown
#4596 Natural
#4754 Landlust Red
#4816 Fuchsia

Knitting Needles:
U.S. size 7 / 4.5 mm

Finished Measurements:
Approx. 21½ in / 55 cm
long, knit to desired
length to fit

PETROL BLUE HEADBAND

GAUGE
17 sts and 32 rows in Pattern Stitch
= 4 x 4 in / 10 x 10 cm

PATTERN STITCH
Rows 1 and 2: Knit.
Rows 3 and 4: Purl.
Rep Rows 1–4 for pattern.

INSTRUCTIONS
CO 20 sts. Work in pattern until
piece measures approx. 21½ in / 55
cm long. Measure around your own
head for fit. BO.

FINISHING

Sew the short ends together using
mattress stitch. At the seam, draw
the ends together as shown in the
photo to create a tuck and stitch in
place. Weave in ends.

STRIPES AND TUCKS HEADBAND

GAUGE
17 sts and 30 rows in seed stitch =
4 x 4 in / 10 x 10 cm

PATTERN STITCH
Seed Stitch (over an odd number of
sts)
Row 1 (RS): K1, (p1, k1) across.
Row 2 (WS): P1, (k1, p1) across.
Rep Rows 1 and 2 for pattern.

INSTRUCTIONS
With any color, CO 19 sts.
Row 1: K1, (p1, k1) to end of row.
Work in Seed Stitch, changing colors as
desired, until piece measures approx.
21½ in / 55 cm long. Measure around
your own head for fit. BO.

FINISHING

Sew the short ends together using
mattress stitch. At the seam, draw the
ends together as shown in the photo to
create a tuck and stitch in place. If
desired, wrap this point with several
strands of yarn or a narrow strip of
stockinette stitch. Weave in ends.

5/6 HAIR TIES

MATERIALS

GRASS-GREEN HAIR TIE
Yarn:
CYCA #4 (worsted/afghan/aran), Landlust Tweed or equivalent (87 yd/80 m / 50 g)

Yarn Amounts:
#4824 Grass Green, 100 g

Knitting Needles:
U.S. size 9 / 5.5 mm

Notions:
Approx. 47¼ in / 120 cm of 3mm craft wire

Finished Measurements:
Approx. 37 in / 94 cm long

PETROL BLUE HAIR TIE
Yarn:
CYCA #4 (worsted/afghan/aran), Landlust Tweed or equivalent (87 yd/80 m / 50 g)

Yarn Amounts:
#4898 Petrol Blue, 50 g

Knitting Needles:
U.S. size 9 / 5.5 mm

Notions:
Approx. 43¼ in / 110 cm of 3mm craft wire

Finished Measurements:
Approx. 37 in / 94 cm long

GRASS-GREEN HAIR TIE

GAUGE
16 sts and 22 rows in St st = 4 x 4 in / 10 x 10 cm

PATTERN STITCH
Stockinette Stitch (St st): Knit RS rows, purl WS rows.

INSTRUCTIONS
CO 30 sts. Work 4 rows in St st, then dec as follows: On the next row then every 4th row 4 more times, dec at beg and end of row—20 sts rem.

Work even until piece measures approx. 33 in / 84 cm, then inc as follows: On the next row then every 4th row 4 more times, inc at beg and end of row—30 sts.

When piece measures approx. 37 in / 94 cm, BO.

FINISHING

Fold the piece in half lengthwise. Sew the BO edge and long edge together. Cut the craft wire and form a loop of about 2 in / 5 cm at each end. Slide the wire inside the headband and close the remaining seam.

PETROL BLUE HAIR TIE

GAUGE
16 sts and 22 rows in St st = 4 x 4 in / 10 x 10 cm

PATTERN STITCH
Stockinette Stitch (St st): Knit RS rows, purl WS rows.

INSTRUCTIONS
CO 20 sts. Work in St st until piece measures approx. 37 in / 94 cm, BO.

FINISHING

Fold the piece in half lengthwise. Sew the BO edge and long edge together. Cut the craft wire and form a loop of about 2 in / 5 cm at each end. Slide the wire inside the headband and close the remaining seam.

7 BLACKBERRY CABLED HAT

MATERIALS

Yarn:
CYCA #4 (worsted/afghan/aran), Landlust Tweed or equivalent (87 yd/80 m / 50 g)

Yarn Amounts:
#4843 Blackberry, 100 g

Knitting Needles:
U.S. size 8 / 5 mm and U.S. size 10 / 6 mm circular needle, 16 in / 40 cm long or dpn

Notions:
Cable needle

Finished Measurements:
Circumference: approx. 21-23 in / 54-58 cm

PATTERN

GAUGE
20 sts and 20 rows in Diamond Pattern with larger needles = 4 x 4 in / 10 x 10 cm

PATTERN STITCHES
Diamond Pattern: See chart.
16-st and 4-st Cable Patterns: See chart.

INSTRUCTIONS
With smaller ndls, CO 102 sts. Join to work in the round being careful not to twist sts. Set up patterns as follows: Work Diamond Pattern over 34 sts, work 16-st Cable Pattern 4 times, work last 4-st Cable Pattern once. (**Note:** The section of cables begins and ends with a 4-st braid.)

Work as set for 6 rnds, then change to larger ndls.

Work as set until hat measures approx. 9 in / 23 cm, then beg dec as follows: On the next rnd, k2tog 4 times over each 8 st cable, decreasing them each to 4 sts and p2tog on each purl column between braids—16 cable sts and 8 purls decreased, 78 sts rem.

Work 1 rnd in patt as set, then k2tog around.

FINISHING

Cut yarn and draw tail through rem sts to fasten off. Pull tails inside and weave in ends.

CHART KEY

P K

Sl 1 st to cn and hold at *back*, k1, k1 from cn

Sl 1 st to cn and hold at *back*, k1, p1 from cn

Sl 4 sts to cn and hold at *front*, k4, k4 from cn

Sl 2 to cn and hold at *front*, k2, k2 from cn

Sl 1 to cn and hold at *front*, k1, k1 from cn

Sl 1 to cn and hold at *front*, p1, k1 from cn

CABLE PATTERN

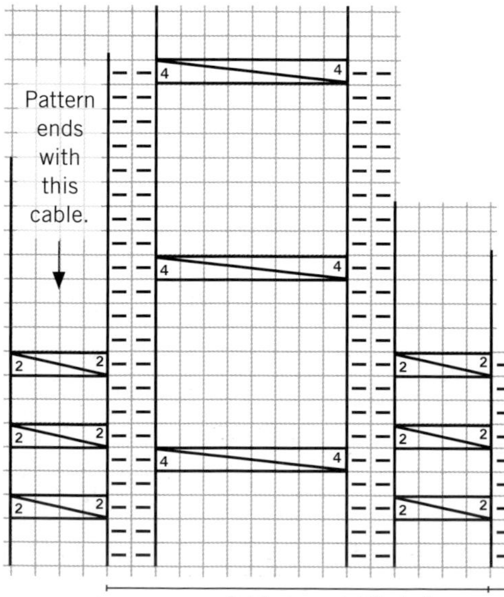
Pattern ends with this cable.

DIAMOND PATTERN

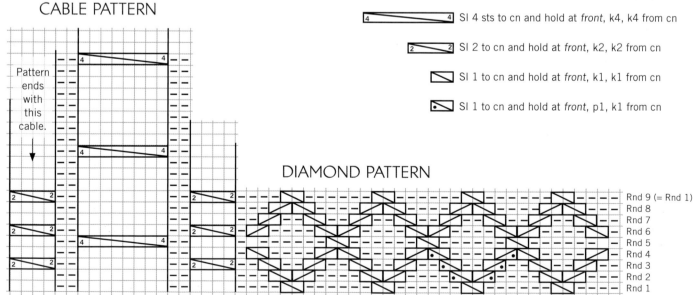

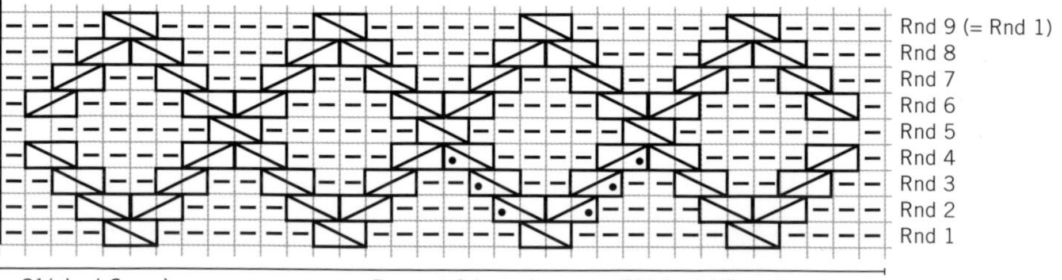
Rnd 9 (= Rnd 1)
Rnd 8
Rnd 7
Rnd 6
Rnd 5
Rnd 4
Rnd 3
Rnd 2
Rnd 1

Cable repeat 16 sts (approx. 2¼ in / 6 cm)

Repeat 34 sts (approx. 7½ in / 19 cm)

8 SLOUCHY ROPE CABLED HAT

PATTERN

GAUGE
17 sts and 21 rows in Cable Pattern with larger needles = 4 x 4 in / 10 x 10 cm

PATTERN STITCHES
Ribbing: (K1, p1) around.
Cable Pattern (see chart): Rep Rnds 1-11 for pattern.

INSTRUCTIONS
With smaller ndls, CO 90 sts. Join to work in the rnd, being careful not to twist sts.
Work 6 rnds in Ribbing, then change to larger ndls. Begin working in Cable Pattern (see chart), and inc 3 sts over each knitted cable panel as follows:
Inc Rnd: *P3, k1, m1, k2, m1, k3, m1, k1; rep from* around.
Work the 13-st repeat 9 times around—117 sts.

After 46 rnds are complete, beg dec as follows:
Next rnd: (P3tog, work 10 sts of cable) around.
Work 2 rnds as set.
Next rnd (after cable crossing rnd): *P1, (k2tog, k2tog, k1) twice; rep from * around.
Work 5 rnds as set.
Next rnd (cable crossing rnd): *P2, (sl3 sts to cn and hold in front, k3, k3 from cn); rcp from * around.
Next rnd: K2tog around.

FINISHING

Cut yarn and draw tail through rem sts to fasten off. Pull tails inside and weave in ends.

MATERIALS

Yarn:
CYCA #4 (worsted/afghan/aran), Landlust Tweed or equivalent (87 yd/80 m / 50 g)

Yarn Amounts:
#2017 Light Gray, 150 g

Knitting Needles:
U.S. size 8 / 5 mm and U.S. size 10 / 6 mm circular needle, 16 in / 40 cm long or dpn

Notions:
Cable needle

Finished Measurements:
Circumference: approx. 21-23 in / 54-58 cm

CABLE CHART

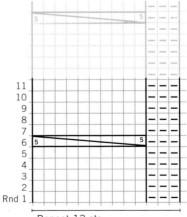

KEY

⊟ P   ☐ K

Sl 5 to cn and hold at front, k5, k5 from cn

Repeat 13 sts
(approx. 2¾ in / 7 cm)

MATERIALS

Yarn:
CYCA #4 (worsted/afghan/aran), Landlust Tweed or equivalent (87 yd/80 m / 50 g)

Yarn Amounts:
#4824 Grass Green, 50 g
#4816 Fuchsia, 50 g
#4754 Landlust Red, 50 g
#4840 Orange, 50 g

Knitting Needles:
U.S. size 7 / 4.5 mm and U.S. size 9 / 5.5 mm circular needle, 16 in / 40 cm long or dpn

Finished Measurements:
Circumference: approx. 20½–22 in / 52–56 cm

9 FUNKY POMPOM HAT

PATTERN

GAUGE

16 sts and 22 rows in rev St st with larger needles = 4 x 4 in / 10 x 10 cm

PATTERN STITCH

Reverse Stockinette Stitch (rev St st): Purl all rnds.
Ribbing: (K1, p1) around.

INSTRUCTIONS

With Grass Green and smaller ndls, CO 86 sts. Join to work in the rnd, being careful not to twist sts. Work in Ribbing until piece measures approx. 1½ in / 4 cm. Change to larger needles and Rev St st, changing colors as follows:
Rnds 1 and 2: Work in Grass Green.
Rnds 3 and 4: Work in Fuchsia.
Rnds 5 and 6: Work in Grass Green.
Rnds 7 and 8: Work in Landlust Red.
Rnds 9 and 10: Work in Grass Green.
Rnds 11 and 12: Work in Orange.
Rep Rnds 1–12 for Stripe Pattern. When piece measures approx. 12 in / 30 cm, BO.

FINISHING

Sew the top of the hat: Lay hat flat and join 1 st from each side 43 times. Make a 2 in 1 5-cm pompom in Fuchsia and another in Orange. Sew pompoms onto the corners of the hat. Weave in ends.

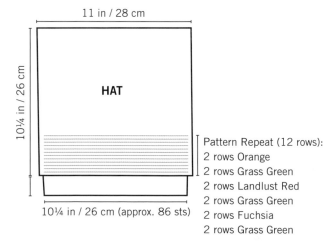

11 in / 28 cm

10¼ in / 26 cm

HAT

10¼ in / 26 cm (approx. 86 sts)

Pattern Repeat (12 rows):
2 rows Orange
2 rows Grass Green
2 rows Landlust Red
2 rows Grass Green
2 rows Fuchsia
2 rows Grass Green

10 GREEN WITH ENVY CROCHETED CAP

MATERIALS

Yarn:
CYCA #4 (worsted/afghan/aran), Landlust Tweed or equivalent (87 yd/80 m / 50 g)

Yarn Amounts:
#4824 Grass Green, 100 g

Crochet Hook:
U.S. size G-6 / 4 mm

Finished Measurements:
Circumference: approx. 22½ in / 57 cm

PATTERN

GAUGE
15 dc and 9 rnds = 4 x 4 in / 10 x 10 cm

PATTERN STITCHES
Main Pattern: Double crochet around.
Band Pattern: Single crochet around.

INSTRUCTIONS
Ch 5. Join chain with sl st to form a ring. Begin working in rnds as follows:

Rnd 1: Ch 3 (counts as first dc), 12 dc in ring, join with sl st.

Rnd 2: Ch 3, 2 dc in each dc around (26 sts), join with sl st.

Rnd 3: Ch 3, (dc in next dc, 2 dc in next dc) around (39 sts), join with sl st.

Rnd 4: Ch 3, (dc in next 2 dc, 2 dc in next dc) around (52 sts), join with sl st.

Rnd 5: Ch 3, (dc in next 4 dc, 2 dc in next dc) around (62 sts), join with sl st.

Rnd 6: Ch 3, (dc in next 6 dc, 2 dc in next dc) around (70 sts), join with sl st.

Rnd 7: Ch 3, (dc in next 10 dc, 2 dc in next dc) around (76 sts), join with sl st.

Rnd 8: Ch 3, (dc in next 9 dc, 2 dc in next dc) around (83 sts), join with sl st.

Rnd 9: Ch 3, (dc in next 8 dc, 2 dc in next dc) around (92 sts), join with sl st.

Rnd 10: Ch 3, (dc in next 8 dc, 2 dc in next dc) around (102 sts), join with sl st.

Rnd 11: Ch 3, (dc in next 8 dc, 2 dc in next dc) around (114 sts), join with sl st.

Rnd 12: Ch 3, (dc in next 8 dc, 2 dc in next dc) around (126 sts), join with sl st.

Rnd 13: Ch 3, dc in each dc around, join with sl st.

Rnd 14: Rep rnd 13.

Rnd 15: Ch 3, (dc in next 5 dc, sk next dc) around (105 sts), join with sl st.

Rnd 16: Ch 3, (dc in next 4 dc, sk next dc) around (84 sts), join with sl st.

Rnd 17: Ch 1, sc around, join with sl st.

Rnd 18: Ch 1, (sc in next 3 sc, sk next sc) around (63 sts), join with sl st.

Rnd 19: Ch 1, (sc in next 4 sc, sk next sc) around (51 sts), join with sl st.

Rnd 20: Ch 1, sc around, join with sl st.

FINISHING

Weave in ends.

MATERIALS

Yarn:
CYCA #4 (worsted/afghan/aran), Landlust Tweed or equivalent (87 yd/80 m / 50 g)

Yarn Amounts:
#4817 Gray Brown, 50 g
#4898 Petrol Blue, 50 g
#4874 Dark Turquoise, 50 g

Knitting Needles:
U.S. size 7 / 4.5 mm circular needle, 16 in / 40 cm long or dpn

Crochet Hook:
U.S. size 7 / 4.5 mm

Finished Measurements:
Circumference: approx. 21–23 in / 54–58 cm

11 CROCHETED TOQUE WITH WIDE STRIPES

PATTERN

GAUGE
14 hdc and 11 rnds = 4 x 4 in / 10 x 10 cm

PATTERN STITCHES
Main Pattern: Hdc (work rounds in spirals without turning chains).
Ribbing: (K2, p2) around.

INSTRUCTIONS
With Gray Brown, ch 4. Join with sl st to form a ring.
Rnd 1: 8 sc in ring. Begin working in hdc as follows:
Rnd 2: 2 hdc in each sc around (16 sts).
Rnd 3: (Hdc in next hdc, 2 hdc in next hdc) around (24 sts).
Rnd 4: (Hdc in next 2 hdc, 2 hdc in next hdc) around (23 sts).
Rnd 5: Hdc around (no increases).
Rnd 6: (Hdc in next 4 hdc, 2 hdc in next hdc) around (38 sts).
Rnd 7: (Hdc in next 5 hdc, 2 hdc in next hdc) around (44 sts).
Rnd 8: (Hdc in next 6 hdc, 2 hdc in next hdc) around (50 sts).
Rnd 9: (Hdc in next 7 hdc, 2 hdc in next hdc) around (56 sts).
Rnds 10 and 11: Hdc around (no increases). Change colors.

Rnd 12: With Petrol Blue, (hdc in next 6 hdc, 2 hdc in next hdc) around (64 sts).
Rnds 13–15: Hdc around (no increases).
Rnd 16: (Hdc in next 7 hdc, 2 hdc in next hdc around (72 sts).
Rnd 18: With Dark Turquoise, hdc around.

Change to circular or double-pointed knitting needles and inc to 84 sts as follows:
(Pick up and knit 1 st in the front loop of next 7 hdc, pick up and knit 1 st in the front loop and 1 st in the back loop of next hdc) around (12 sts increased).

Rnds 18–23: Work in Ribbing.
BO.

FINISHING

Weave in ends.

12 CROCHETED TOQUE WITH NARROW STRIPES

PATTERN

GAUGE
10 hdc and 11 rnds = 4 x 4 in / 10 x 10 cm

PATTERN STITCHES
Main Pattern: Hdc around. (Hint: In each rnd, work the hdc sts between the hdc sts of the previous rnd to create a spiral pattern, working in the round without joining or working a turning chain.)
Ribbing: (K2, p2) around.

INSTRUCTIONS
With Dark Brown, ch 5. Join with sl st to form a ring.
Rnd 1: 9 sc in ring. Begin working in hdc as follows:
Rnd 2: 2 hdc in each sc around (18 sts).
Rnd 3: Hdc after next hdc on prev rnd, 2 hdc after next hdc (27 sts).
Rnd 4: Hdc after next 2 hdc on prev rnd, 2 hdc after next hdc (36 sts). Change to Rose.
Rnd 5: With Rose, hdc around (36 sts).
Rnd 6: Hdc after next 3 hdc on prev rnd, 2 hdc after next hdc (45 sts). Change to Medium Gray.
Rnd 7: With Medium Gray, hdc around. Change to Dark Brown.
Rnd 8: With Dark Brown, (hdc after next 4 dc on prev rnd, 2 hdc after next hdc) (54 sts).
Continue without increasing as follows:
Rnd 9: With Rose, hdc around. Change to Medium Gray.

Rnds 10 and 11: With Medium Gray, hdc around. Change to Dark Brown.
Rnd 12: With Dark Brown, hdc around. Change to Rose.
Rnd 13: With Rose, hdc around. Change to Medium Gray.
Rnd 14: With Medium Gray, hdc around. Change to Dark Brown.
Rnds 15 and 16: With Dark Brown, hdc around. Change to Rose.
Rnds 17 and 18: With Rose, hdc around. Change to Medium Gray.
Rnd 19: With Medium Gray, hdc around. Change to Dark Brown.
Rnds 20 and 21: With Dark Brown, hdc around. Change to Rose.

Change to circular or double-pointed knitting needles and inc to 76 sts as follows:
(Pick up and knit 1 st in the next hdc, pick up and knit 1 st in the front loop and 1 st in the back loop of next hdc) twice (pick up and knit 1 st in the next hdc, pick up and knit 1 st in the front loop and 1 st in the back loop of next hdc, pick up and knit 1 st in the next 2 hdc, pick up and knit 1 st in the front loop and 1 st in the back loop of the next hdc) 10 times (22 sts increased).

Work 6 rnds in Ribbing. BO.

FINISHING

Weave in ends.

MATERIALS

Yarn:
CYCA #4 (worsted/afghan/aran), Landlust Tweed or equivalent (87 yd/80 m / 50 g)

Yarn Amounts:
#4741 Dark Brown, 50 g
#4854 Rose, 50 g
#4742 Medium Gray, 50 g

Knitting Needles:
U.S. size 7 / 4.5 mm circular needle, 16 in / 40 cm long or dpn

Crochet Hook:
U.S. size H-8 / 5 mm

Finished Measurements:
Circumference: approx. 20½–22 in / 52–56 cm

MATERIALS

Yarn:
CYCA #4 (worsted/afghan/aran), Landlust Tweed or equivalent (87 yd/80 m / 50 g)

Yarn Amounts:
#4824 Grass Green or #4715 Dark Green, 150 g

Knitting Needles:
U.S. size 6 / 4 mm circular needle, 16 in / 40 cm long

Notions:
3 buttons to fit buttonholes, sewing needle and matching thread

Finished Measurements:
13½ in / 34 cm x 23½ in / 60 cm

13 WEATHER THE STORM SHAWL COLLAR

PATTERN

GAUGE
18 sts and 22 rows in Ribbing = 4 x 4 in / 10 x 10 cm

PATTERN STITCHES
Ribbing: (K2, p2) around.

INSTRUCTIONS
CO 102 sts. Work in Ribbing for 2¾ in / 7 cm as follows:
Work selvage st, (k2, p2) across to last 3 sts, k2, work selvage st.
When piece measures 2¾ in / 7 cm, make the first buttonhole as follows:
Work selvage st, k2, yo, p2tog, work across row as set.
Continue in pattern as set making 2 more buttonholes after working 2¾ in / 7 cm from the last buttonhole.
When piece measures approx. 13¼ in / 34 cm, BO.

COLLAR diagram

23½ in / 60 cm

13½ in / 34 cm

COLLAR

K2 P2 Ribbing

Direction of Knitting

2¾ in / 7 cm   2¾ in / 7 cm   2¾ in / 7 cm

102 sts

FINISHING
Sew on buttons. Weave in ends.

14 OUTRAGEOUSLY CUTE WRIST WARMERS

PATTERN

GAUGE
17 sts and 24 rows in St st = 4 x 4 in / 10 x 10 cm

PATTERN STITCHES
Stockinette Stitch (St st): Knit all rnds.
Reverse stockinette stitch (rev St st): Purl all rnds.

INCREASES AND DECREASES
Increases: At the beginning of the 1st and 3rd ndls, k2tog.
Decreases: At the beginning of the 1st and 3rd ndls, k1, m1 (insert the left ndl under the bar between sts from front to back and knit into the back of that loop).

INSTRUCTIONS
With Natural, CO 32 sts and divide the sts evenly on dpn. Join to work in the round, being careful not to twist sts.
Rnds 1–5: With Natural, knit. Change to Yellow Green.
Rnd 6: With Yellow Green, knit.
Rnds 7–9: Purl. Change to Natural.
Rnds 10–12: With Natural, knit. Change to Green.
Rnd 13: With Green, knit.
Rnds 14–16: Purl. Change to Natural.
Rnds 17–19: With Natural, knit. Change to Dark Green.
Rnd 20: With Dark Green, knit.
Rnds 21–23: Purl. Change to Natural.
Rnds 24–26: With Natural, knit. Change to Green.
Rnd 27: With Green, knit and dec 2 sts (30 sts).

Rnds 28–30: Purl. Change to Natural.
Rnds 31–33: With Natural, knit. Change to Yellow Green.
Rnd 34: With Yellow Green, knit and dec 2 sts (28 sts).
Rnds 35–37: Purl. Change to Dark Brown.
Rnds 38–40: With Dark Brown, knit. Change to Green.
Rnd 41: With Green, knit.
Rnds 42–44: Purl. Change to Dark Brown.
Rnds 45–47: With Dark Brown, knit. Change to Dark Green.
Rnd 48: With Dark Green, knit and inc 2 sts (30 sts).
Rnds 49–51: Purl. Change to Dark Brown.

Continue the stripe pattern as follows: Beginning with the 3rd rnd of Dark Brown, inc in the following Green and Yellow Green stripes (34 sts). Then, repeating stripe pattern without increases, follow diagram as a guide. When all stripes are complete, BO.

Work the second cuff the same way.

FINISHING

Weave in ends.

MATERIALS

Yarn:
CYCA #4 (worsted/afghan/aran), Landlust Tweed or equivalent (87 yd/80 m / 50 g)

Yarn Amounts:
#4596 Natural, 20 g
#4885 Yellow Green, 20 g
#4756 Green, 20 g
#4715 Dark Green, 20 g
#4741 Dark Brown, 20 g

Knitting Needles:
U.S. size 8 / 5 mm

Finished Measurements:
Approx. 4¾ x 9½ in / 12 x 24 cm, measured unstretched

5 rnds Natural
3 rnds Yellow Green
3 rnds Natural
4 rnds Green
3 rnds Natural
4 rnds Dark Green
3 rnds Natural
4 rnds Green
3 rnds Natural
4 rnds Yellow Green
3 rnds Dark Brown
4 rnds Green
3 rnds Dark Brown
4 rnds Dark Green ← Center of cuff
3 4nds Dark Brown
4 rnds Green
3 rnds Dark Brown
4 rnds Yellow Green
3 rnds Natural
4 rnds Green
3 rnds Natural
4 rnds Dark Green
3 rnds Natural
3 rnds Green
3 rnds Natural
4 rnds Yellow Green
5 rnds Natural

MATERIALS

Yarn:
CYCA #4 (worsted/afghan/
aran), Landlust Tweed or
equivalent (87 yd/80 m /
50 g)

Yarn Amounts:
#4824 Grass Green, 50 g
#4814 Plum, 50 g
#4840 Orange, 50 g
#4816 Fuchsia, 50 g
#4715 Dark Green, 50 g

Knitting Needles:
U.S. size 8 / 5 mm

Finished Measurements:
Approx. 6¼ in / 16 cm
circumference x 10¼ in /
26 cm long, without
fringe

15 FABULOUS FRINGED WRIST WARMERS

PATTERN

GAUGE
17 sts and 24 rows in rev St st =
4 x 4 in / 10 x 10 cm

PATTERN STITCH
Reverse stockinette stitch (rev St st):
Purl RS rows, knit WS rows.

INSTRUCTIONS
With Grass Green, CO 44 sts. Work in
rev St st and change colors as follows:
* Work 2 rows in Grass Green, 2 rows
in Plum, 2 rows in Orange, 2 rows in
Fuchsia, and 2 rows in Dark Green.
Repeat from * 3 more times (a total of
4 stripe pattern repeats).

Cut the yarn after each 2-row stripe,
leaving tails about 3 in / 8 cm long to
form fringes later. Do not carry the
unused color(s) up the side.

When cuff measures approx. 6½ in /
16 cm, BO.

Work the second cuff the same way.

FINISHING

Sew the CO and BO edges together,
leaving an opening for the thumb (see
diagram). Tie the tails left from the
stripes to form fringes. Trim if desired.
Wash and dry flat to block.

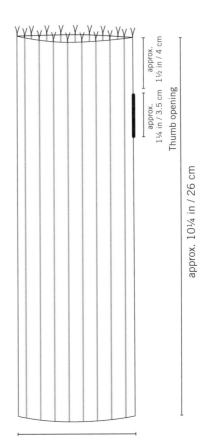

approx. 1½ in / 4 cm

approx. 1¼ in / 3.5 cm

Thumb opening

approx. 10¼ in / 26 cm

approx. 3 in / 8 cm

REPEAT
2 rows Dark Green
2 rows Fuchsia
2 rows Orange
2 rows Plum
2 rows Grass Green

16 COMFY CABLED WRIST WARMERS

PATTERN

GAUGE
17 sts and 25 rows in St st = 4 x 4 in / 10 x 10 cm

PATTERN STITCHES
Stockinette Stitch (St st): Knit RS rows, purl WS rows.
Reverse Stockinette Stitch (rev St st): Purl RS rows, knit WS rows.
Ribbing: (K1, p1) across.
Eyelet Pattern: P1, yo, p2tog, p1, yo, p2tog, p1, yo, p2tog.

INSTRUCTIONS
Left Cuff
With smaller ndls, CO 32 sts. Work in Ribbing for approx. ¾ in / 2 cm.
Change to larger ndls. Set up columns of St st and rev St st as follows:
Row 1 (RS): K20, p9, k3 (32 sts).
Row 2 (WS): P2, k9, p20.
Row 3: K20, (p2, p2tog, yo, p1, yo, p2tog, p2), k3.
Continue in patts as set and in the purl section, beginning 6 rows above the ribbing, work Eyelet pattern every 6th row(see Pattern Stitches).
At the same time, inc as follows: On the 14th, 32nd and 50th rows, m1 after the first st and before the last st of the row (38 sts).

When piece measures approx. 11 in / 28 cm, end after a WS row.
Next row (RS): Rep Row 3.
Change to smaller ndls. Work in Ribbing for approx. ½ in / 1 cm.
BO.

Right Cuff
Work as for left cuff, reversing shaping. That is, work Row 1 as follows to reverse position of patterns:
Row 1 (RS): K3, p9, k20 (32 sts).

Laces (make 2)
With larger ndls, CO 5 sts and work in St st until piece measures approx. 40 in / 100 cm. Put sts on waste yarn in case the length needs to be changed.

FINISHING

Thread the laces through the eyelets using the diagram as a guide. Adjust the length of the laces if needed and BO. Sew ends to inside of glove.
Sew side seam leaving an opening for the thumb, using the diagram as a guide.
Weave in ends. Wash and dry flat to block.

MATERIALS

Yarn:
CYCA #4 (worsted/afghan/aran), Landlust Tweed or equivalent (87 yd/80 m / 50 g)

Yarn Amounts:
#4816 Fuchsia, 100 g

Knitting Needles:
U.S. size 7 and 8 / 4.5 mm and 5 mm

Finished Measurements:
Approx. 4¾ in / 12 cm wide x 11½ in / 29 cm long

Lacing Diagram

approx. 3½ in / 9 cm

approx. ¾ in / 2 cm

approx. 1½ in / 4 cm

approx. 2 in / 5 cm Thumb Opening

approx. 11½ in / 29 cm

approx. ½ in / 1 cm

approx. 4¾ in / 12 cm

17/18/19 BOOT TOPPERS

MATERIALS

LANDLUST RED CUFFS

Yarn:
CYCA #4 (worsted/afghan/aran),
Landlust Tweed or equivalent
(87 yd/80 m / 50 g)

Yarn Amounts:
#4754 Landlust Red, 50 g

Knitting Needles:
U.S. size 8 / 5 mm short
circular needle or dpn

Finished Measurements:
Approx. 6 x 6 in / 15 x 15 cm,
measured unstretched

JACQUARD CUFFS

Yarn:
CYCA #4 (worsted/afghan/aran),
Landlust Tweed or equivalent
(87 yd/80 m / 50 g)

Yarn Amounts:
#4805 Turquoise, 50 g
#4817 Gray Brown, 50 g

Knitting Needles:
U.S. size 8 / 5 mm short
circular needle or dpn

Notions:
Cable needle or spare double-
pointed needle

Finished Measurements:
Approx. 5½ x 5 in / 14 x 13 cm

GRASS GREEN CUFFS

Yarn:
CYCA #4 (worsted/afghan/aran),
Landlust Tweed or equivalent
(87 yd/80 m / 50 g)

Yarn Amounts:
#4824 Grass Green, 50 g

Knitting Needles:
U.S. sizes 8 and 9 / 5 mm and
5.5 mm short circular needles
or dpn

Finished Measurements:
Approx. 6 x 6 in / 15 x 15 cm,
measured unstretched

LANDLUST RED CUFFS

GAUGE
1 cable repeat of 10 sts =
2½ in / 6 cm

PATTERN STITCHES
Ribbing: (K2, p2) around.
Cable: See chart.

INSTRUCTIONS
CO 55 sts. Join to work in the round
being careful not to twist sts.
Rnds 1–8: Work in Ribbing.
Rnd 9 (inc rnd): (K7, m1) 6 times,
k2—50 sts.
Begin Cable Pattern with Row 2 of
chart as follows:
Rnd 10: (K8, p2) 5 times around.
Rnd 11: Work charted patt as set.
Rnd 12: On Row 3 of chart, work cable
crossing as follows: Sl 2 to cn and hold
in back, k2, k2 from cn, sl 2 to cn and
hold in front, k2, k2 from cn.
Rnds 13–22: Work as set until all rnds
of cable chart have been completed
once, then work Rows 1–11 of chart
once more.
Rnd 23 (dec rnd): (P6, p2tog) 6 times,
p2—44 sts.
Rnds 24–36: Work in Ribbing.
BO.
Make second cuff the same way.

FINISHING

Weave in ends.

CABLE CHART

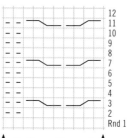

12
11
10
9
8
7
6
5
4
3
2
Rnd 1

↑ Pattern Repeat ↑

KEY

☐ K   – P

Sl 2 to cn and hold in *front*, k2, k2 from cn

Sl 2 to cn and hold in *back*, k2, k2 from cn

BOOTIE CUTIE CUFFS

GAUGE
18 sts and 24 rows in Color Pattern = 4 x 4 in / 10 x 10 cm

PATTERN STITCHES
Ribbing: (K1, p1) around.
Eyelet Rnd: (K2tog, yo) around.
Color Pattern: see chart.

INSTRUCTIONS
With Turquoise, CO 48 sts. Join to work in the rnd being careful not to twist.
Rnds 1–14: Work in Ribbing.
Rnd 15 (eyelet rnd): (K2tog, yo) around.
Rnd 16: Knit.
Rnds 17–29: Work Color Pattern (see chart). When working long stretches in one color, catch floats on back of work every 3 sts.
Rnd 30: Knit.
Rnds 31–40: Work in Ribbing.
BO.
Make second cuff the same way.

FINISHING

Weave in ends.

GOING GREEN CUFFS

GAUGE
14 sts and 22 rows in Blackberry Stitch = 4 x 4 in / 10 x 10 cm

PATTERN STITCHES
Ribbing: (K2, p2) around.
Blackberry Stitch: Repeat Rnds 7–10 of instructions for patt.

INSTRUCTIONS
With smaller ndls, CO 44 sts. Join to work in the round, being careful not to twist.
Rnds 1–6: Work in Ribbing. Change to larger ndls and begin working in Blackberry Stitch as follows:
Rnd 7: *(K1, p1, k1) in the next st, p3tog; rep from * 10 more times, 11 repeats total (44 sts).
Rnd 8: Knit.
Rnd 9: *P3tog, (k1, p1, k1) in the next st; rep from * 10 more times.
Rnd 10: Knit.
Rnds 11–18: Rep Rnds 7–10 2 more times, 3 repeats total. Change to smaller ndls.
Rnds 19–30: Work in ribbing.
BO.
Work second cuff the same way.

FINISHING

Weave in ends. Turn cuffs inside out so the proper side of the pattern is on the outside.

COLOR CHART

☐ Turquoise ● Gray Brown

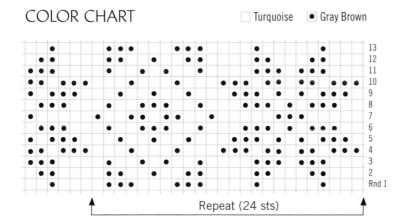

Repeat (24 sts)

MATERIALS

(for 1 pair)
Yarn:
CYCA #4 (worsted/afghan/aran), Landlust Tweed or equivalent (87 yd/80 m / 50 g)

Yarn Amounts:
Total approx. 50 g in different colors: #4715 Dark Green, #4885 Yellow Green, #4741 Dark Brown, #4898 Petrol Blue, #2017 Light Gray, #4805 Turquoise, #4596 Natural, #4802 Rust, #4752 Landlust Red

Knitting Needles:
U.S. size 7 and 8 / 4.5 and 5 mm

Crochet Hook:
U.S. size 7 and H-8 / 4.5 and 5 mm

Finished Measurements:
Knit to desired size

20 STEP IT UP SHOE INSOLES

PATTERN

GAUGE
17 sts and 24 rows in St st with larger needles = 4 x 4 in / 10 x 10 cm

PATTERN STITCH
Stockinette Stitch (St st): Knit RS rows, purl WS rows.

INSTRUCTIONS
Before beginning, make an outline of your foot. Use this to determine how many stitches you need to cast on and knit in the chosen color pattern until the piece is the desired length. Work in any colors to your liking and begin the color pattern at the desired location.

FINISHING

Work 1 rnd of sc around the outside edge of the insole. Weave in ends.

For extra warmth, make 2 insoles for each foot and crochet or sew them together to form a double-thick insole.

CHART 1

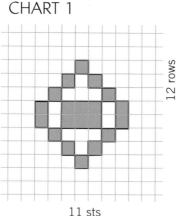

12 rows

11 sts

■ Yellow Green

□ Dark Green

CHART 2

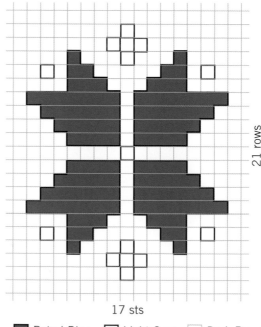

21 rows

17 sts

■ Petrol Blue   □ Light Gray   □ Dark Brown

CHART 3

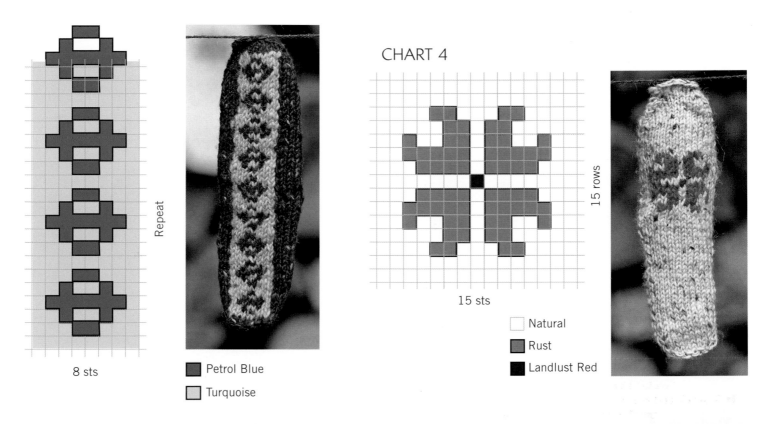

Repeat

8 sts

■ Petrol Blue
□ Turquoise

CHART 4

15 rows

15 sts

□ Natural
■ Rust
■ Landlust Red

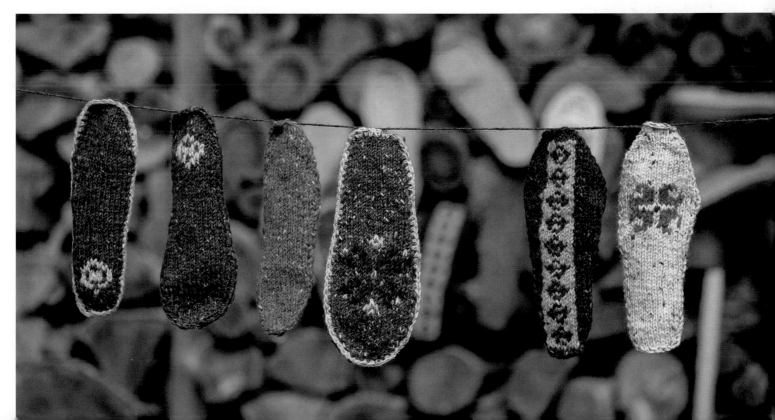

SWEATERS AND VESTS

22
BACK TO CLASSICS JACKET

23
DOWN TO EARTH CABLED PULLOVER

24
FLATTERING BUTTONED CORSET

25
STRIKING LACED CORSET

26
JACQUARD CORSET

27
DRAPING
HOODED
PULLOVER

28
PLAID PONCHO

FATHER & SON
BOYS' VEST

30

29 FATHER &
SON MEN'S
PULLOVER

"FATHER & SON"

MATERIALS

Yarn:
CYCA #4 (worsted/afghan/
aran), Landlust Tweed or
equivalent (87 yd/80 m /
50 g)

Yarn Amounts:
#4843 Blackberry, 550
(600, 650, 700) g

Knitting Needles:
U.S. size 7 and 9 / 4.5 and
5.5 mm straight or circular
needles

Size:
S (M, L, XL)

Finished Measurements:
Bust: 38 (41, 44, 47) in /
96 (104, 112, 120) cm
Length: 24½ (24¾, 25½,
26) in / 62 (63, 64, 65) cm

PATTERN

GAUGE
14 sts and 24 rows in Moss Stitch with
larger needles = 4 x 4 in / 10 x 10 cm

PATTERN STITCHES
Moss Stitch
Row 1 (RS): (K1, p1) across.
Rows 2 and 4: Work the sts as they
appear (k the knits and p the purls).
Row 3: (P1, k1) across.
Rep Rows 1–4 for patt.

Ribbing: (K1tbl, p1) across

Lace Pattern: See chart. Only RS rows
are shown. On WS rows, work the sts as
they appear (k the knits and p the
purls). Rep Rows 1–8 for pattern. 1
repeat measures approx. 6 in / 15 cm
wide.

21 BOPPING AROUND TOWN PULLOVER

Decorative Decreases
On RS rows, at the beg of the row work
k2tog over the 2nd and 3rd sts and at
the end of the row work k2tog-tbl on
the 2nd and 3rd sts from the end.

INSTRUCTIONS
Back
With smaller ndls, CO 85 (91, 97,
103) sts. Work in Ribbing for 1½ in / 4
cm. Change to larger ndls and set up
patts as follows:
Next row: Work selvage st, work 3 (6,
9, 12) sts in Moss Stitch, work Sts
1–26 of Lace Pattern (see chart) twice,
then work Sts 1–25 of Lace Pattern
once more, work 3 (6, 9, 12) sts in
moss stitch, work selvage stitch.
Cont in patts as set until piece
measures approx. 16½ in / 42 cm. End
after a WS row.

Armhole Shaping
BO 3 (3, 4, 5) sts at beg of next 2
rows, then BO 2 (3, 3, 3) sts at beg of
next 2 rows. Then, using Decorative
Decreases, dec 1 st at beg and end of
every other row 6 times. When the
decreases reach the Lace Pattern, work

the first and last 10 sts of Lace panel
as St st.

Cont in patts as set until piece
measures 23½ (24, 24½, 24¾) in /
60 (61, 62, 63) cm.

Neck Shaping
BO center 17 sts. Work both sides
separately.
On the left side every other row, BO 5
sts at the neck edge twice. When piece
measures 24½ (24¾, 25, 25½) in /
62 (63, 64, 65) cm, BO rem 24 (27,
30, 33) shoulder stitches.
Re-attach yarn to right shoulder and
work as for left shoulder, reversing
shaping.

Front
With smaller ndls, CO 85 (91, 97,
103) sts. Work in Ribbing for 1½ in / 4
cm. Change to larger ndls and set up
patts as follows:
Next row: Work selvage st, work 3 (6,
9, 12) sts in Moss Stitch, work Sts
1–26 of Lace Pattern (see chart) twice,
then work Sts 1–25 of Lace Pattern
once more, work 3 (6, 9, 12) sts in

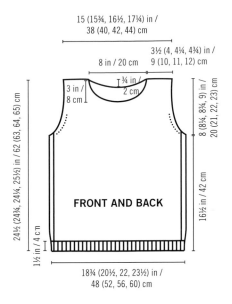

FRONT AND BACK

15 (15¾, 16½, 17¼) in / 38 (40, 42, 44) cm

3½ (4, 4¼, 4¾) in / 9 (10, 11, 12) cm

8 in / 20 cm

¾ in / 2 cm

3 in / 8 cm

8 (8¼, 8¾, 9) in / 20 (21, 22, 23) cm

24¼ (24¾, 24¼, 25½) in / 62 (63, 64, 65) cm

16½ in / 42 cm

1½ in / 4 cm

18¾ (20½, 22, 23½) in / 48 (52, 56, 60) cm

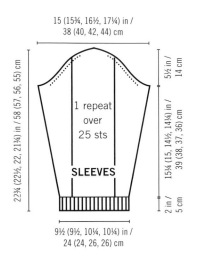

SLEEVES

15 (15¾, 16½, 17¼) in / 38 (40, 42, 44) cm

1 repeat over 25 sts

5½ in / 14 cm

15¼ (15, 14½, 14¼) in / 39 (38, 37, 36) cm

22¾ (22½, 22, 21½) in / 58 (57, 56, 55) cm

2 in / 5 cm

9½ (9½, 10¼, 10¼) in / 24 (24, 26, 26) cm

LACE CHART

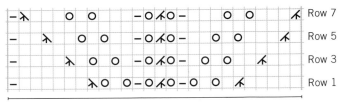

Repeat 26 sts
3rd repeat ends with k 6 (2 x 26 sts + 1 x 25 sts = 77 sts total)

KEY

⅄ Sl 1, k2tog, psso

⋏ K3tog

O Yarn over

— P on RS, k on WS

☐ K on RS, p on WS

---

moss stitch, work selvage stitch. Cont in patts as set until piece measures approx. 16½ in / 42 cm. End after a WS row.

Armhole Shaping

BO 3 (3, 4, 5) sts at beg of next 2 rows, then BO 2 (3, 3, 3) sts at beg of next 2 rows. Then, using Decorative Decreases, dec 1 st at beg and end of every other row 6 times. When the decreases reach the Lace Pattern, work the first and last 10 sts of Lace panel as St st.

Cont in patts as set until piece measures 21¼ (21½, 22, 22½) in / 54 (55, 56, 57) cm.

Neck Shaping

BO center 9 sts. Work both sides separately.

On the left side, every other row at neck edge, BO 5 once, then BO 3 sts once, then BO 2 sts twice, then dec 1 st twice. When piece measures 24½ (24¾, 25, 25½) in / 62 (63, 64, 65) cm, BO rem 24 (27, 30, 33) shoulder stitches.

Re-attach yarn to right shoulder and work as for left shoulder, reversing shaping.

Sleeves

With smaller ndls, CO 43 (43, 45, 45) sts. Work in Ribbing for 2 in / 5 cm. Change to larger ndls and set up patts as follows:

Next row: Work selvage st, work 8 (8, 9, 9) sts in Moss Stitch, work sts 1–25 of Lace Pattern once (end with k6), work 8 (8, 9, 9) sts in Moss Stitch, work selvage stitch.

Work 16 (8, 8, 8) rows in patts as set then inc beg and end of every 8th row (alternating every 8th and 6th rows, every 8th row, every 6th row) 8 (10, 11, 13 times) — 59 (63, 67, 71) sts total.

Work even until piece measures 17¼ (17, 16½, 16) in / 44 (43, 42, 41) cm.

Cap Shaping

At beg of next 2 rows BO 4 sts once, then at beg of following 2 rows BO 2 (3, 4, 5) sts once.

Then dec 1 st at beg and end of every

other row 14 times—19 (21, 23, 25) sts rem.

When piece measures 22¾ (22½, 22, 21½) in / 58 (57, 56, 55) cm, BO.

Make second sleeve the same way.

FINISHING

Pin out pieces to dimensions shown on schematic. Dampen and allow to dry. Sew shoulder, side, and underarm seams. Set sleeves into armhole. Neckband: With smaller ndls, pick up and knit 78 sts around neck (34 sts across back and 44 sts across front), and work Ribbing for 1¼ in / 3 cm. BO. Weave in ends.

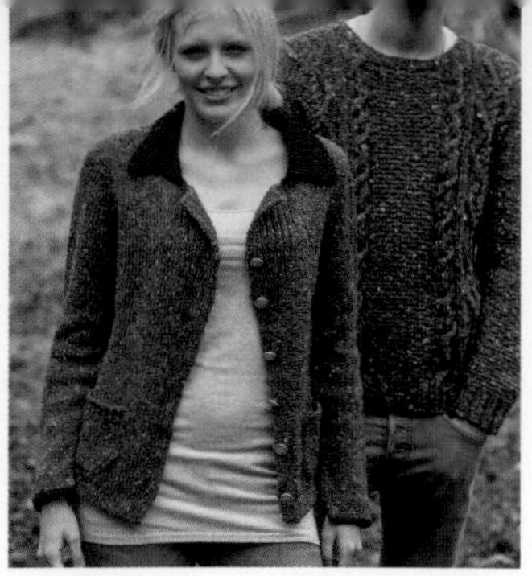

MATERIALS

Yarn:
CYCA #4 (worsted/afghan/aran), Landlust Tweed or equivalent (87 yd/80 m / 50 g)

Yarn Amounts:
#4741 Dark Brown, 550 (600, 650, 700) g
#4754 Landlust Red, 50 (50, 100, 100) g

Knitting Needles:
U.S. sizes 7, 9, and 11 / 4.5 mm, 5.5 mm, and 8 mm straight or circular needles

Notions:
6 buttons, sewing needle and matching thread

Size:
S (M, L, XL)

Finished Measurements:
Bust: 36¼ (39½, 42½, 45½) in / 92 (100, 108, 116) cm
Length: 23½ (24, 24½, 25) in / 60 (61, 62, 63) cm

22 BACK TO CLASSICS JACKET

PATTERN

GAUGE
16 sts and 22 rows in St st with U.S. size 9 / 5.5 mm needles = 4 x 4 in / 10 x 10 cm

PATTERN STITCHES
Stockinette Stitch (St st): Knit on RS, purl on WS.
Ribbing: (K1, p1) across.
DECORATIVE DECREASES
On RS rows, at the beg of the row work k2tog and at the end of the row work k2tog-tbl.

INSTRUCTIONS
Back
With Dark Brown and U.S. size 7 / 4.5 mm ndls, CO 70 (74, 78, 82) sts. Work 8 rows in St st.
Next row (RS, foldline): With U.S. size 11 / 8 mm ndls, knit.
Next row: With U.S. size 7 / 4.5 mm ndls, purl.
Change to U.S. size 9 / 5.5 mm ndls; cont in St st and inc as follows:
Next row (RS): *K14 (14, 15, 16), m1; rep from * across—74 (78, 82, 86) sts.
Work even until piece measures 4¾ in / 12 cm from the foldline.

Waist Shaping
Dec every 6th row 4 times, on the RS, as follows: K3, k2tog, knit to last 5 sts, k2tog-tbl, k3.
Then inc every 6th row 4 times, on the RS, as follows: k4, m1, knit to last 4 sts, m1, k4—74 (78, 82, 86) sts after last inc row.
Work even until piece measures 15¾ in / 40 cm.

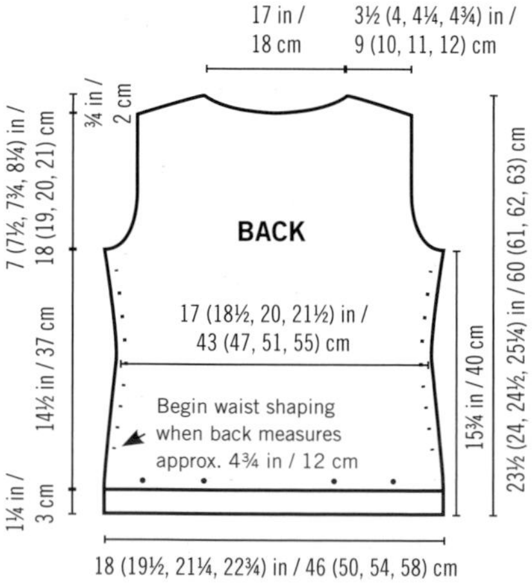
17 in / 18 cm
3½ (4, 4¼, 4¾) in / 9 (10, 11, 12) cm
¾ in / 2 cm
7 (7½, 7¾, 8¼) in / 18 (19, 20, 21) cm
BACK
18 cm
17 (18½, 20, 21½) in / 43 (47, 51, 55) cm
14½ in / 37 cm
Begin waist shaping when back measures approx. 4¾ in / 12 cm
15¾ in / 40 cm
23½ (24, 24½, 25¼) in / 60 (61, 62, 63) cm
1¼ in / 3 cm
18 (19½, 21¼, 22¾) in / 46 (50, 54, 58) cm

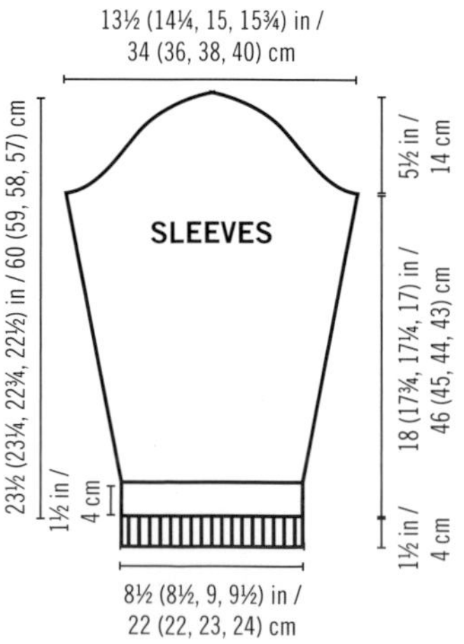
13½ (14¼, 15, 15¾) in / 34 (36, 38, 40) cm
SLEEVES
23½ (23¼, 22¾, 22½) in / 60 (59, 58, 57) cm
5½ in / 14 cm
18 (17¾, 17¼, 17) in / 46 (45, 44, 43) cm
1½ in / 4 cm
1½ in / 4 cm
8½ (8½, 9, 9½) in / 22 (22, 23, 24) cm

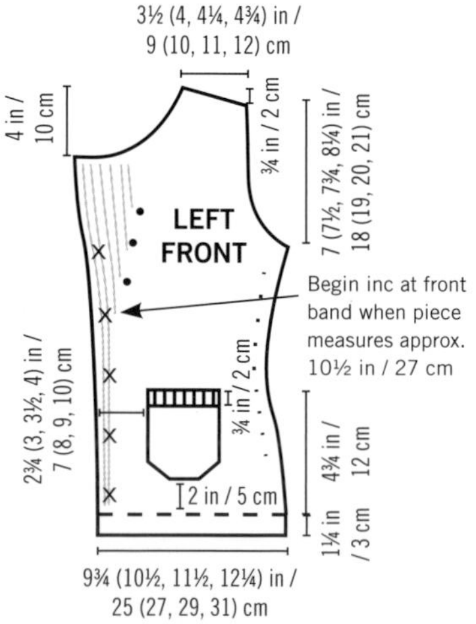
3½ (4, 4¼, 4¾) in / 9 (10, 11, 12) cm
4 in / 10 cm
¾ in / 2 cm
7 (7½, 7¾, 8¼) in / 18 (19, 20, 21) cm
LEFT FRONT
Begin inc at front band when piece measures approx. 10½ in / 27 cm
2¾ (3, 3½, 4) in / 7 (8, 9, 10) cm
¾ in / 2 cm
4¾ in / 12 cm
2 in / 5 cm
1¼ in / 3 cm
9¾ (10½, 11½, 12¼) in / 25 (27, 29, 31) cm

KEY
- When piece measures 14¼ (14½, 15, 15¼) in / 36 (37, 38, 39) cm, inc before the first purl on the lapel on the next row then every 8th row twice.
- × Buttonhole

Armhole Shaping

BO 3 (3, 4, 4) sts at beg of next 2 rows, then BO 2 (2, 3, 3) sts at beg of next 2 rows. Then dec 1 st at beg and end of every other row 4 (5, 4, 5) times—56 (58, 60, 62) sts.
Work even until piece measures 23 (23¼, 23½, 24) in / 58 (59, 60, 61) cm.

Neck and Shoulder Shaping

BO center 18 sts. Work both sides separately.
On the left side every other row at the neck edge, BO 4 sts once then BO 2 sts once. *At the same time*, shape shoulders as follows: at the shoulder edge, BO 5 (5, 6, 6) sts twice.
Tip for experts: You can use short-row shaping for the shoulders.
BO rem 3 (4, 3, 4) sts.
Re-attach yarn to right shoulder and work as for left shoulder, reversing shaping.

Left Front

With Dark Brown and smallest ndls, CO 36 (39, 42, 45) sts. Work 8 rows in St st.
Next row (RS, foldline): With largest ndls, knit.
With smallest ndls, work 7 more rows in St st.
Next row (RS): CO 6 sts for button placket, knit across—42 (45, 48, 51) sts.
Next row (WS): Work selvage st, (p1, k1) 3 times, p34 (37, 40, 43) sts, work selvage st.
Change to medium ndls and on opposite edge from button placket, work waist shaping as for back.

Lapel Shaping

When piece measures approx. 10½ (11, 11½, 11¾) in / 27 (28, 29, 30) cm, add more ribbing to the lapel section as follows:
Next row (RS): Work selvage st, k32 (35, 38, 41), (k1, p1) 4 times, work selvage st.
Work 7 rows as set.
Next row (RS): Work selvage st, k30, (33, 35, 39), (k1, p1) 5 times, work selvage st.
Rep last 8 rows 3 more times, working one more (k1, p1) each time.
Continue as set until piece measures

14¼ (14½, 15, 15¼) in / 36 (37, 38, 39) cm.
On the next row then every 8th row 2 more times: Before the first purl on the lapel, m1.
Work even until piece measures 15¾ in / 40 cm.

Armhole Shaping

Every other row, at the armhole edge, BO 3 (3, 4, 4) sts once, then BO 2 (2, 3,3) sts once, then dec every other row 4 (5, 4, 5) times—58 (58, 60, 62) sts.
Work even until piece measures 19¾ (20, 20¼, 20½) in / 50 (51, 52, 53) cm. End after a RS row.

Neck and Shoulder Shaping

BO the 14 sts of the lapel at beg of next row (WS). Then every other row at the neck edge, BO 3 sts twice then dec 1 st 3 times.
When neck measures 3 in / 8 cm, shape shoulders as follows:
Every other row, at the shoulder edge, BO 5 (5, 6, 6) sts twice.
Tip for experts: You can use short-row shaping for the shoulders.
BO rem sts.

Right Front

Work as for left front, reversing shaping and making buttonholes as follows:
On a RS row, work 3 sts in patt, k2tog, yo, work remainder of row in patt. Make first buttonhole when piece measures 2 in / 5 cm, then make 5 more buttonholes 2¼ in / 6 cm apart. For the 6th buttonhole, work 5 sts in patt, k2tog, yo, work remainder of row in patt.

Sleeves

With Landlust Red and U.S. size 7 / 4.5 mm ndls, CO 39 (40, 42, 44) sts. Work 8 rows in Ribbing.
Next row (RS, foldline): Work with U.S. size 11 / 8 mm ndls.
Work 7 more rows with U.S. size 7 / 4.5 mm ndls, alternating rows of Dark Brown and Landlust Red for stripes.
Change to U.S. size 9 / 5.5 mm ndls and St st.
Work even until piece measures 4 (3, 2½, 2½) in / 10 (8, 6, 6) cm from fold line, then inc at beg and end of every 10th (8th, 8th, 8th) row 8 (9, 10, 11) times—55 (58, 62, 66) sts.
Work even until piece measures 18

(17¾, 17½, 17) in / 46 (45, 44, 43) cm.

Cap Shaping

At beg of next 2 rows BO 3 (3, 4, 4) sts once, then at beg of following 2 rows BO 3 (3, 4, 4) sts once. Then dec 1 st at beg and end of every other row 12 times, then BO 2 sts at beg of next 2 rows twice.
When piece measures 23½ (23¼, 23, 22¾) in / 60 (59, 58, 57) cm, BO rem 13 (14, 16, 18) sts.

Make second sleeve the same way.

Pockets

With Dark Brown and U.S. size 7 / 4.5 mm ndls, CO 21 sts. Work 6 rows in K1, P1 Ribbing as follows: Work selvage st, (k1, p1) 8 times, k1, work selvage st.
Change to U.S. size 9 / 5.5 mm ndls and work 18 rows in St st.
For bottom of pocket, dec beg and end of every other row 4 times.
BO rem sts.

Make second pocket the same way.

FINISHING

Pin out pieces to dimensions shown on schematic. Dampen and allow to dry. Sew shoulder seams. Sew side and sleeve seams, sewing the first 1¼ in / 3 cm on the WS for hem. Fold hem up on all pieces and sew in place. Set sleeves into armholes. Sew pockets in place using diagram as a guide. Sew on buttons. Weave in ends.

Collar

With Landlust Red and U.S. size 7 / 4.5 mm ndls, pick up and knit 65 sts around neck (25 sts on back and 20 sts on each front, beginning after the first buttonhole and ending before the last so the collar is between the lapel ribbing sections). Work in K1, P1 Ribbing as follows: Work selvage st, p1, (k1, p1) to last st, work selvage st.

When piece measures 2 in / 5 cm, inc at beg and end of next 2 RS rows, then when piece measures 3 in (7½) cm, inc at beg and end of next 2 RS rows—73 sts.
When piece measures 4 in / 10 cm, BO.

MATERIALS

Yarn:
CYCA #4 (worsted/afghan/ aran), Landlust Tweed or equivalent (87 yd/80 m / 50 g)

Yarn Amounts:
#4741 Dark Brown, 700 (750, 800) g

Knitting Needles:
U.S. sizes 7 and 9 / 4.5 mm and 5.5 mm straight or circular needles, short circular needle for neckband

Notions:
Cable needle

Size:
S (M, L)

Finished Measurements:
Chest: 44 (47¼, 50) in / 112 (120, 128) cm
Length: 27½ (28, 28½) in / 70 (71, 72) cm

23 DOWN TO EARTH CABLED PULLOVER

PATTERN

GAUGE
15 sts and 21 rows in Texture Pattern with larger needles = 4 x 4 in / 10 x 10 cm

PATTERN STITCHES
Texture Pattern (see Chart A): Multiple of 4+1. RS and WS rows are charted. Repeat Sts 1–4 across row, then end with St 5 to center pattern. Repeat Rows 1–4 for pattern.
Ribbing: (K2, p2) across.
Cable Pattern (see Chart B): Only RS rows are charted. On WS rows, work the sts as they appear (k the knits and p the purls). Work Rows 1–20 once, then rep Rows 5–20 for pattern.
Braid Pattern: See Chart C.

INSTRUCTIONS
Back
With smaller ndls, CO 90 (100, 106) sts. Work in Ribbing for 2½ in / 6 cm. Change to larger ndls. On the next row, m1 after every 10th st and, *at the same time*, set up patts as follows:
Work selvage st, 9 (13, 17) sts in Texture Pattern, 33 sts in Cable and Braid Patterns, 17 sts in Texture Pattern, 33 sts in Braid and Cable Patterns (reverse positions of cables), 9 (13, 17) sts in Texture Pattern, work selvage st—103 (109, 115) sts.
Work as set until piece measures 19 in / 48 cm.

Shape Armhole
BO 3 (4, 5) st at beg of next 2 rows, then BO 2 sts at beg of next 2 rows, then dec at beg and end of every other row 4 times—85 (89, 93) sts.
Work as set until piece measures 26¾ (27, 27¼) in / 68 (69, 70) cm.

Neck and Shoulder Shaping
BO center 23 sts. Work both sides separately.
On the left side, every other row at neck edge, BO 5 (6, 7) sts once then BO 3 sts once.
Work as set until piece measures 26¾ (27, 27¼) in / 70 (71, 72) cm.
BO rem sts for shoulder.
Re-attach yarn to right shoulder and work as for left shoulder, reversing shaping.

Front
With smaller ndls, CO 90 (100, 106) sts. Work in Ribbing for 2½ in / 6 cm. Change to larger ndls. On the next row, m1 after every 10th st and, *at the same time*, set up patts as follows:
Work selvage st, 9 (13, 17) sts in Texture Pattern, 33 sts in Cable and Braid Patterns, 17 sts in Texture Pattern, 33 sts in Braid and Cable Patterns (reverse positions of cables), 9 (13, 17) sts in Texture Pattern, work selvage st—103 (109, 115) sts.
Work as set until piece measures 19 in / 48 cm.

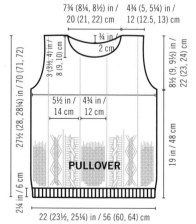

17¼ (18, 19) in / 44 (46, 48) cm

7¾ (8¼, 8½) in / 20 (21, 22) cm   4¾ (5, 5¼) in / 12 (12.5, 13) cm

¾ in / 2 cm

3 (3½, 4) in / 8 (9, 10) cm

8½ (9, 9½) in / 22 (23, 24) cm

5½ in / 14 cm   4¾ in / 12 cm

27½ (28, 28¼) in / 70 (71, 72) cm

19 in / 48 cm

PULLOVER

2¼ in / 6 cm

22 (23½, 25¼) in / 56 (60, 64) cm

1.) TEXTURE PATTERN

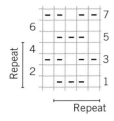

2.) CABLE PATTERN   3.) BRAID PATTERN

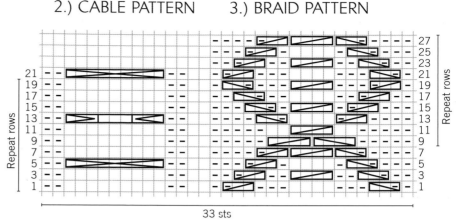

33 sts

Repeat rows = as marked

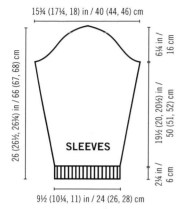

15¾ (17¼, 18) in / 40 (44, 46) cm

6¼ in / 16 cm

19½ (20, 20½) in / 50 (51, 52) cm

26 (26½, 26¾) in / 66 (67, 68) cm

SLEEVES

2¾ in / 6 cm

9½ (10¼, 11) in / 24 (26, 28) cm

Shape Armhole

BO 3 (4, 5) st at beg of next 2 rows, then BO 2 sts at beg of next 2 rows, then dec beg and end of every other row 4 times—85 (89, 93) sts.
Work as set until piece measures 24 in / 62 cm.

Neck and Shoulder Shaping

BO center 13 sts. Work both sides separately.
On the left side every other row at the neck edge, BO 4 (5, 6) sts once then BO 2 sts twice, then dec 1 st 5 times.
Work as set until piece measures 26¾ (27, 27¼) in / 70 (71, 72) cm.
BO rem sts for shoulder.
Re-attach yarn to right shoulder and work as for left shoulder, reversing shaping.

Sleeves

With smaller ndls, CO 44 (48, 52) sts.
Work 6 rows in Ribbing.
Change to larger ndls and Texture Pattern and on the first row, inc 1 st somewhere in the middle of the row—45 (49, 53) sts.

Work even until piece measures 5½ (5, 4¼) in / 14 (13, 11) cm, then inc at beg and end of every 10th row 7 (8, 9) times—59 (65, 71) sts.
Work even until piece measures 19½ (20, 20½) in / 50 (51, 52) cm.

Cap Shaping

At beg of next 2 rows BO 4 (4, 5) sts once, then at beg of following 2 rows BO 3 (4, 4) sts once. Then dec 1 st at beg and end of every other row 16 times.
When piece measures 26 (26½, 26¾) in / 66 (67, 68) cm, BO rem sts.

Make second sleeve the same way.

FINISHING

Pin out pieces to dimensions shown on schematic. Dampen and allow to dry. Sew shoulder, side, and underarm seams. Set sleeves into armhole.
Neckband: With smaller ndls, pick up and knit 72 (76, 80) sts around neck—32 (34, 36) sts across back and 40 (42, 44) sts across front—and work in the round in Ribbing for 1¼ in / 3 cm. BO.
Weave in ends.

KEY

─ P   ☐ K

Sl 2 to cn and hold in *front*, k2, k2 from cn

Sl 2 to cn and hold in *back*, k2, k2 from cn

Sl 2 to cn and hold in *front*, p1, k2 from cn

Sl 1 to cn and hold in *back*, k2, p1 from cn

Sl 3 to cn and hold in *back*, sl 3 to second cn and hold in *front*, k3, k3 from second cn, k3 from first cn

Sl 6 to cn and hold in *back*, k3, move the last 3 sts on cn back onto the left ndl, k3, k3 from cn

MATERIALS

Yarn:
CYCA #4 (worsted/afghan/aran), Landlust Tweed or equivalent (87 yd/80 m / 50 g)

Yarn Amounts:
#4582 Stone Gray, 250 g

Knitting Needles:
U.S. sizes 7 and 8 / 4.5 mm and 5 mm

Crochet Hook:
U.S. size H-8 / 5 mm

Notions:
6 buttons, sewing needle and matching thread

Size:
S (M, L, XL)

Finished Measurements:
Bust: 34½ (37, 39½, 41¾) in / 88 (94, 100, 106) cm
Length: 17¾ (18, 19, 19½) in / 45 (46, 48, 50) cm

PATTERN

GAUGE
17 sts and 27 rows in St st with larger needles = 4 x 4 in / 10 x 10 cm

PATTERN STITCHES
Stockinette Stitch (St st): Knit on RS, purl on WS.
Reverse Stockinette Stitch (rev St st): Purl on RS, knit on WS.
Ribbing: (K1, p1) across.
Crochet Edging: Work 1 row of sc, then work 1 row of crab stitch (reverse sc) from left to right.

EYELET PANEL
Row 1 (RS): P9.
Row 2 (WS): K9.
For largest size only, rep Rows 1 and 2 once more.

24 FLATTERING BUTTONED CORSET

Next row (2-Eyelet Row): P2, p2tog, yo, p1, yo, p2tog, p2.
Work 7 rows even.
Next row (3-Eyelet Row): P1, yo, (p2tog, p1, yo) twice, p2tog.
Rep last 8 rows 12 (12, 12, 13) more times.
Work 3 (3, 3, 5) rows even.
Repeat 2-Eyelet Row once more.

DECORATIVE DECREASES
Left-Leaning Decrease: Sl 1 knitwise, k1, psso.
Right-Leaning Decrease: K2tog.

INSTRUCTIONS
Back
With smaller ndls, CO 76 (82, 86, 94) sts. Work in Ribbing for ¾ in / 2 cm. Change to larger ndls and St st.

Waist Shaping
When piece measures 2 (2, 2¼, 2¼) in / 5 (5, 6, 6) cm (see schematic), begin waist shaping with Decorative Decreases as follows:
Next row (RS): Knit 12 (12, 13, 13); sl 1, k1, psso; knit to last 14 (14, 15, 15) sts; k2tog; knit to end.
Rep dec row every 4th row 4 more times—66 (72, 76, 84) sts rem.
When piece measures 4¾ (4¾, 5, 5) in / 12 (12, 13, 13) cm (see schematic), begin waist increases as follows:
Next row (RS): Knit 12 (12, 13, 13), M1, knit to last 12 (12, 13, 13) sts, M1, knit to end.
Repeat inc row every 4th row 2 more times then every 6th row twice—76 (82, 86, 94) sts.
When piece measures 9¼ (9½, 10¼, 10½) in / 24 (25, 26, 27) cm, begin armhole shaping.

Armhole Shaping
BO 3 (4, 4, 5) sts at beg of next 2 rows; then, using Decorative Decreases, dec 2 sts from the edge at beg and end of every RS row 6 (7, 7, 8) times.
When piece measures 14½ (15, 15¾, 15¾) in / 37 (38, 40, 40) cm, begin neck shaping.

Neck Shaping
BO center 20 (22, 22, 22) sts.
Then, working each side with a separate ball of yarn, BO every other row at the neck edge as follows: BO 3 sts once, then BO 2 sts once, then dec 1 st at neck edge every other row 5 times—9 (9, 11, 13) sts rem in each shoulder.
When piece measures 17¾ (18, 18¾, 19½) in / 45 (46, 48, 50) cm, BO rem sts at shoulder.

Left Front (as worn)
With smaller ndls, CO 38 (41, 44, 47) sts. Work in Ribbing for ¾ in / 2 cm. Change to larger ndls and set up patts as follows:
Row 1 (setup row, RS): Work selvage st, k 11 (13, 14, 15) sts, p1, k 5 (5, 6, 6), pm, work Eyelet Panel over next 9 sts, pm, k 4 (4, 4, 5), work selvage st.
Continue as set in panels of St st separated by purls and Eyelet Panel between markers, and when piece measures 2 (2, 2¼, 2¼) in / 5 (5, 6, 6) cm (see schematic), begin waist shaping with Decorative Decreases as follows:
Next row (dec row, RS): Work selvage st, knit to last 2 sts before first purl, k2tog, p1, k 5 (5, 6, 6), work Eyelet Panel between markers, k 4 (4, 4, 5), work selvage st.
Continue in patts as set and rep dec row every 4th row 4 more times.

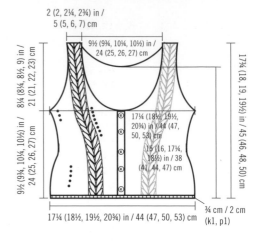

2 (2, 2¼, 2¾) in / 5 (5, 6, 7) cm

9½ (9¾, 10¼, 10½) in / 24 (25, 26, 27) cm

8¼ (8¼, 8½, 9) in / 21 (21, 22, 23) cm

17¾ (18, 19, 19½) in / 45 (46, 48, 50) cm

9½ (9¾, 10¼, 10½) in / 24 (25, 26, 27) cm

17¼ (18½, 19½, 20¾) in / 44 (47, 50, 53) cm

15 (16, 17¼, 18½) in / 38 (41, 44, 47) cm

17¼ (18½, 19½, 20¾) in / 44 (47, 50, 53) cm

¾ cm / 2 cm (k1, p1)

When piece measures 5 (5½, 6, 6) in / 13 (14, 15, 15) cm (see schematic), begin bust shaping as follows:

Next row (inc row, RS): Work as set to last stitch of Eyelet Panel, slip 2nd marker, M1, work as set to end of row.

Continue in patts as set and rep inc row every 4th row 7 more times—you will now have 13 (14, 15, 16) knit sts in panel between Eyelet Panel and next purl column. *At the same time*, on the row with the second-to-last increase (see diagram), begin decreases every RS row **3 times as follows:** Work to last 2 sts before the first purl, k2tog, continue in patts as set—38 (41, 44, 47 sts) after all increases and decreases are complete.

Work even in patts as set until piece measures 9½ (10, 10¼, 10½) in / 24 (25, 26, 27) cm.

Armhole and Neck Shaping

For armhole, at the beg of RS rows, BO 3 (4, 4, 5) sts once, then work sl 1, k1, psso to dec 2 sts from the edge as on back 7 (8, 9, 8) times. *At the same time*, for neck at beg of WS rows, BO 12 (13, 13, 14) sts once, then BO 3 sts once, then BO 2 sts once, then work k2tog 2 sts from the edge as on back twice—9 (9, 11, 13) sts rem.

Size S, M, L: 1 selvage st, 7 (7, 9) purls, 1 selvage st.

Size XL: 1 selvage st, 1 knit, 9 purls, 1 knit, 1 selvage st.

When piece measures 17¾ (18, 19, 19½) in / 45 (46, 48, 50) cm, BO rem sts for shoulder.

Right Front

Work as for Left Front, reversing position of pattern sts and shaping as follows:

Row 1 (setup row, RS): Work selvage st, k4 (4, 4, 5), pm, work Eyelet Panel over next 9 sts, pm, k5 (5, 6, 6), p1, k 11 (13, 14 15), work selvage st.

Waist Decreases: Work sl 1, k1, psso on the first 2 sts after the last purl column.

Bust Increases: Work M1 before first marker for Eyelet Panel.

Underarm Decreases: Work sl 1, k1, psso on the first 2 sts after the last purl column.

Underarm Shaping: Begin on WS rows and work decs as k2tog.

Neck Shaping: Begin on RS rows and work decs as sl 1, k1, psso.

2 Cable Bands

For each cable band, CO 5 sts and work in St st for approx. 71 (75, 78, 83) in / 180 (190, 200, 210) cm. BO.

FINISHING

Except for the cable bands, pin out pieces to dimensions shown on schematic. Dampen and allow to dry. Sew side seams and shoulder seams.

With crochet hook, work 1 round of sc and 1 round of crab stitch (reverse sc) around armholes. Work 1 row of sc and one row of crab stitch around neckline and front opening, making 6 button-holes evenly spaced along right-front edge.

Lace the cable bands through the eyelets using the diagram as a guide. Adjust the length of the bands if needed and BO. Sew ends to inside of vest. Sew buttons on left front to correspond with buttonholes.

LEFT FRONT SHAPING DETAIL
(Size S shown)

9 sts (purl on RS)

Dec 1 st every other row 7 times at armhole edge

BO 3 sts

BO at neck edge every other row

1 st twice
2 sts once
3 sts once
12 sts once

Dec 1 st every other row 3 times as follows: k2tog using the 2 sts to the right of the purl section

Inc every 4th row

	K2tog
6th and 7th sts	every
7th and 8th sts	other row
8th and 9th sts	as follows:
9th and 10th sts	
10th and 11th sts	

K4   K5   K5   K11

1 selvage st   P1   P9   P1   1 selvage st

38 sts total

Ribbing (k1, p1)

MATERIALS

Yarn:
CYCA #4 (worsted/afghan/
aran), Landlust Tweed or
equivalent (87 yd/80 m /
50 g)

Yarn Amounts:
#4843 Blackberry, 200
(300, 350, 400) g

Knitting Needles:
U.S. sizes 7 and 8 / 4.5 mm
and 5 mm

Crochet Hook:
U.S. size H-8 / 5 mm

Notions:
Ribbon or string for lacing

Size:
S (M, L, XL)

Finished Measurements:
Bust: 34½ (37, 39½, 41¾)
in / 88 (94, 100, 106) cm
17¼ (17¾, 18½, 18½) in /
44 (45, 47, 47) cm

25 STRIKING LACED CORSET

PATTERN

GAUGE
17 sts and 27 rows in St st with larger
needles = 4 x 4 in / 10 x 10 cm

PATTERN STITCHES
Stockinette Stitch (St st): Knit on RS,
purl on WS.
Reverse Stockinette Stitch (rev St st):
Purl on RS, knit on WS.
Ribbing: (K1, p1) across.
Crochet Edging: Work 1 row of sc, then
work 1 row of crab stitch (reverse sc) from
left to right.

EYELET PANEL
Row 1 (RS): P9.
Row 2 (WS): K9.
Rep Rows 1 and 2 another 1 (0, 1, 0)
times.
Next row (2-Eyelet Row): P2, p2tog, yo,
p1, yo, p2tog, p2.
Work 7 rows even.
Next row (3-Eyelet Row): P1, yo, (p2tog,
p1, yo) twice, p2tog.
Rep last 8 rows 12 (12, 12, 13) more
times.
Work 5 (3, 5, 3) rows even.
Repeat 2-Eyelet Row once more.

DECORATIVE DECREASES
Left-Leaning Decrease: Sl 1 knitwise, k1,
psso.
Right-Leaning Decrease: K2tog.

INSTRUCTIONS
Back
With smaller ndls, CO 76 (82, 86, 94)

sts. Work in Ribbing for ¾ in / 2 cm.
Change to larger ndls and St st.

Waist Shaping
When piece measures 2 (2, 2¼, 2¼) in /
5 (5, 6, 6) cm (see schematic), begin
waist shaping with Decorative Decreases
as follows:
Next row (RS): Knit 10 (10, 11, 11); sl
1, k1, psso; knit to last 12 (12, 13, 13)
sts; k2tog; knit to end.
Rep dec row every 4th row 4 more
times—66 (72, 76, 84) sts rem.
When piece measures 5 (5½, 6, 6) in /
13 (14, 15, 15) cm (see schematic),
begin waist increases as follows:
Next row (RS): Knit 12 (12, 13, 13), M1,
knit to last 12 (12, 13, 13) sts, M1, knit
to end.
Repeat inc row every 4th row 2 more times
then every 6th row twice—76 (82, 86, 94)
sts.
When piece measures 9¼ (9¼, 9½,
10¼) in / 24 (24, 25, 26) cm, begin
armhole shaping.

Armhole Shaping
BO 3 (4, 4, 5) sts at beg of next 2 rows;
then, with Decorative Decreases, dec 2
sts from the edge at beg and end of every
RS row 6 (7, 7, 8) times as follows:
Dec row: Work selvage st, k1; sl 1, k1,
psso; work to last 4 sts; k2tog; k1, work
selvage st.
When piece measures 14 (14½, 15,
15¾) in / 36 (37, 38, 40) cm, begin
neck shaping.

Neck Shaping

BO center 20 (22, 22, 22) sts.

Then, working each side with a separate ball of yarn, BO every other row at the neck edge as follows: BO 3 sts once, then BO 2 sts once, then dec 1 st at neck edge every other row 5 times—9 (9, 11, 13) sts rem in each shoulder.

When piece measures 17¼ (17¾, 18½, 18½) in / 44 (45, 47, 47) cm, BO rem sts at shoulder.

Left Front (as worn)

With smaller ndls, CO 34 (36, 39, 44) sts. Work in Ribbing for ¾ in / 2 cm. Change to larger ndls and set up patts as follows:

Row 1 (setup row, RS): Work selvage st, k 20 (21, 23, 26), work Eyelet Panel over next 9 sts, pm, k 3 (4, 5, 7), work selvage st.

Continue as set in St st with Eyelet Panel between markers, and when piece measures 2 (2, 2¼, 2¼) in / 5 (5, 6, 6) cm (see schematic), begin waist shaping with Decorative Decreases as follows:

Next row (dec row, RS): Work selvage st, k8 (9, 10, 11), k2tog, knit to marker, work Eyelet Panel between markers, knit to last st, work selvage st.

Continue in patts as set and rep dec row every 4th row 4 more times.

When piece measures 5 (5½, 6, 6) in / 13 (14, 15, 15) cm (see schematic), begin bust shaping as follows:

Next row (inc row, RS): Work as set to last stitch of Eyelet Panel, slip 2nd marker, M1, work as set to end of row.

Continue in patts as set and rep inc row every 4th row 5 more times—you will now have 9 (10, 11, 13) knit sts in panel between Eyelet Panel and the selvage. Work even in patts as set until piece measures 9 (9¼, 9½, 10¼) in / 23 (24, 25, 26) cm.

Armhole and Neck Shaping

For armhole, at the beg of RS rows, BO 3 (4, 4, 5) sts once, then work sl 1, k1,

psso to dec 2 sts from the edge as on back 7 (8, 9, 8) times.

At the same time, when piece measures 9¼ (9½, 10¼, 10½) in / 24 (25, 26, 27) cm, for neck at beg of WS rows, BO 9 (10, 10, 11) sts once, then work k2tog 2 sts from the edge as on back until the 9 (9, 11, 13) sts with the Eyelet Panel rem.

Size S, M, L: 1 selvage st, 7 (7, 9) purls, 1 selvage st.

Size XL: 1 selvage st, 1 knit, 9 purls, 1 knit, 1 selvage st.

When piece measures 17¼ (17¾, 18½, 19¼) in / 44 (45, 47, 49) cm, BO rem sts for shoulder.

Right Front

Work as for left front, reversing position of pattern sts and shaping as follows:

Row 1 (setup row, RS): Work selvage st, k3 (4, 5, 7), pm, work Eyelet Panel over next 9 sts, pm, k20 (21, 23, 26), work selvage st.

Waist Decreases: Work sl 1, k1, psso on the first 2 sts after the last purl column.

Bust Increases: Work M1 before first marker for Eyelet Panel.

Underarm Decreases: Work sl 1, k1, psso before the last k8 (9, 10, 11) sts of the row.

Underarm Shaping: Begin on WS rows and work decs as k2tog.

Neck Shaping: Begin on RS rows and work decs as sl 1, k1, psso.

Center Front Panel

CO 16 (18, 20, 24) sts and work in rev St st for 9 (9¼, 9½, 10¼) in / 23 (24, 25, 26) cm cm. BO. On the bottom edge, with crochet hook work 1 row of sc and 1 row of crab stitch (reverse sc). (The top edge will be worked later with the neckline of the vest.)

2 Cable Bands

For each cable band, CO 5 sts and work in St st for approx. 71 (75, 78, 83) in / 180 (190, 200, 210) cm. BO.

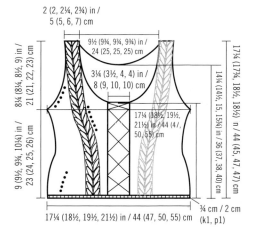

FINISHING

Except for the cable bands, pin out pieces to dimensions shown on schematic. Dampen and allow to dry. Sew side seams and shoulder seams.

With the purl side of the Center Front Panel facing up, place the panel between the two front pieces. Crochet the fronts to the panel with 1 row of sc then work 1 row of crab stitch (reverse sc) across.

With crochet hook, work 1 round of sc and 1 round of crab stitch (reverse sc) around armholes. Work 1 row of sc and one row of crab stitch around neckline and front opening, making 6 buttonholes evenly spaced along right-front edge.

Lace the cable bands through the eyelets, using the diagram on page 59 as a guide. Adjust the length of the bands if needed and BO. Sew ends to inside of vest.

Lace the ribbon up over the Center Front Panel, making crossings at 8 points evenly spaced up the front. Tighten the ribbon as desired to accentuate the waist shaping.

MATERIALS

Yarn:
CYCA #4 (worsted/afghan/aran), Landlust Tweed or equivalent (87 yd/80 m / 50 g)

Yarn Amounts:
#4756 Green, 150 (200, 150, 200, 250) g
#4802 Rust, 150 (200, 150, 200, 250) g

Knitting Needles:
U.S. size 8 / 5 mm

Crochet Hook:
U.S. size H-8 / 5 mm

Notions:
5 buttons, sewing needle and matching thread

Size:
S (M, L, XL)

Finished Measurements:
Circumference: 34¼ (37, 39¼, 43¼) in / 88 (94, 100, 110) cm
Length: 17¼ (17¾, 18½, 18½) in / 44 (45, 47, 47) cm

26 JACQUARD CORSET

PATTERN

GAUGE
18 sts and 23 rows in St st = 4 x 4 in / 10 x 10 cm

PATTERN STITCHES
Stockinette Stitch (St st): Knit on RS, purl on WS.
Crochet Edging: work 1 row of sc, then work 1 row of crab stitch (reverse sc) from left to right.

DECORATIVE DECREASES
Left-Leaning Decrease: Sl 1 knitwise, k1, psso.
Right-Leaning Decrease: K2tog.

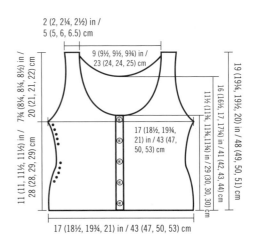

COLOR PATTERN CHART

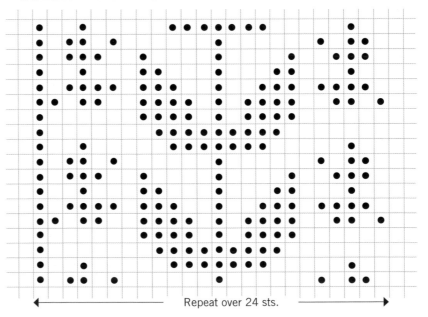

Repeat over 24 sts.

INSTRUCTIONS

Back

With Green, CO 78 (86, 92, 98) sts. Work 2 rows in St st. On row 3 (RS), begin working Color Pattern (see chart), centering pattern on piece.

Waist Shaping

When piece measures 2 (2, 2¼, 2¼) in / 5 (5, 6, 6) cm (see schematic), continue working color pattern and begin waist shaping with Decorative Decreases as follows:

Next row (RS): K2; sl 1, k1, psso; knit to last 4 sts; k2tog; knit to end.
Rep dec row every 4th row 4 more times, then work 4 (4, 6, 6) rows even. Begin waist increases as follows:
Next row (RS): Knit 3, M1, knit to last 3 sts, M1, knit to end.
Repeat inc row every 4th row 2 more times then on the 6th row once, then on the 8th row once—78 (86, 92, 98) sts. When piece measures 11 (11, 11½, 11½) in / 28 (28, 29, 29) cm, begin armhole shaping.

Armhole Shaping

BO 3 (4, 4, 5) sts at beg of next 2 rows; then, with Decorative Decreases, dec 2 sts from the edge at beg and end of every RS row 6 (7, 7, 8) times (on the right edge sl 1, k1, psso and on the left edge k2tog).
When piece measures 16 (16½, 17, 17¼) in / 41 (42, 43, 44) cm, begin neck shaping.

Neck Shaping

BO center 20 (22, 22, 22) sts.
Then working each side with a separate ball of yarn, BO every other row at the neck edge as follows: BO 6 (6, 7, 7) sts once, BO 3 sts once, then BO 2 sts once—9 (9, 11, 13) sts rem in each shoulder.
When piece measures 19 (19¼, 19½, 20) in / 48 (49, 50, 51) cm, BO rem sts at shoulder.

Left Front (as worn)

With Green, CO 39 (43, 46, 59) sts and knit 2 rows. On Row 3 (RS), begin working Color Pattern (see chart), centering pattern on piece.
Continue working Color Pattern, and when piece measures 2 (2, 2¼, 2¼) in / 5 (5, 6, 6) cm (see schematic), begin waist shaping with Decorative Decreases as follows:
Next row (RS): Knit to last 4 sts, k2tog, knit to end.
Rep dec row every 4th row 4 more times, then work 4 (4, 6, 6) rows even. Begin waist increases as follows:
Next row (RS): Knit to last 3 sts, M1, knit to end.
Repeat inc row every 4th row 2 more times then on the 6th row once, then on the 8th row once—39 (43, 46, 59) sts. When piece measures 11 (11, 11½, 11½) in / 28 (28, 29, 29) cm, begin armhole shaping.

Armhole and Neck Shaping

For armhole, at the beg of RS rows, BO 3 (4, 4, 5) sts once, then work sl 1, k1, psso to dec 2 sts from the edge as on back 7 (8, 9, 8) times.
At the same time, when piece measures 11½ (11½, 12, 12) in / 29 (29, 30, 30) cm, for neck at beg of WS rows, BO 10 (10, 11, 11) sts once, then BO 3 sts once, then BO 2 sts once—9 (11, 12, 13) sts rem.

When piece measures 19 (19¼, 19½, 20) in / 48 (49, 50, 51) cm, BO rem sts for shoulder.

Right Front

Work as for left front, reversing shaping as follows:
Waist shaping: Work decreases and increases after the first 2 sts of the row.
Armhole shaping: Work at beg of WS rows and use k2tog for decreasing.
Neck shaping: Work at beg of RS rows.

FINISHING

Pin out pieces to dimensions shown on schematic. Dampen and allow to dry. Sew side seams and shoulder seams. With green and crochet hook work 1 row of sc and 1 row of crab stitch (reverse sc) along the lower edge, around the neck, and around each armhole.
Front Bands: Work 1 row of sc and 1 row of crab stitch on front edges, and on the right front, make 5 buttonholes evenly spaced. Sew buttons onto left front to correspond to buttonholes.

Tip: If you want the corset to be slightly fluffier and softer to the touch, you can lightly felt it. Wet the corset and put it in the dryer for at least 20 minutes; check every 10 minutes. After about 20–30 minutes, the surface should be slightly felted. If you plan to felt the vest, make sure to felt your swatch first. The vest may shrink up to 25 percent when felting, so work a larger size.

MATERIALS

Yarn:
CYCA #4 (worsted/afghan/
aran), Landlust Tweed
or equivalent
(87 yd/80 m / 50 g)

Yarn Amounts:
#4816 Fuchsia, 1150 g

Knitting Needles:
U.S. size 8 / 5 mm

Notions:
2 cable needles, spare
needle or scrap yarn

Size:
One Size

Finished Measurements:
Bust: 37¾ in / 96 cm
Length (without hood):
18 in / 46 cm

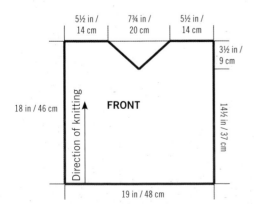

27 DRAPING HOODED PULLOVER

PATTERN

GAUGE
18 sts and 24 rows in St st = 4 x 4 in /
10 x 10 cm

PATTERN STITCHES
Stockinette Stitch (St st): Knit RS
rows, purl WS rows.
Reverse Stockinette Stitch (rev St st):
Purl RS rows, knit WS rows.
Cable Pattern (see chart): Sl 10 sts to
first cn and hold at front; sl 7 sts to 2nd
cn and hold at back, k10, p 7 from 2nd
cn, k10 from first cn. Only RS rows are
charted. On WS rows, work the sts as
they appear (k the knits and p the
purls).

INSTRUCTIONS
Back
CO 155 sts and set up patts as follows:
Work selvage st, p6, 141 sts in Cable
Pattern (following chart), p6, work
selvage st. Work 112 rows in patts as
set.
BO.

Front
Work as for back until piece measures
14½ in / 37 cm (approx. 88 rows).

Neck Shaping
Work 76 sts in patts as set, k2tog; put
rem 77 sts on spare ndl or scrap yarn.
Turn.
Next row (WS): K2tog, work 75 sts in
patts as set (following chart).
Cont to dec every row at neck edge
another 17 times.
When 112 rows are complete, BO rem
59 sts.

Return held sts to ndls and work
second shoulder, reversing shaping.

Hood
CO 115 sts and set up patts as follows:
K2, p4, work 103 sts as charted
(between A and B), p4, k2.
Work Rows 1–104 of chart once, then
Rows 25–112 once. When approx. 192
rows are complete, BO.

Sleeves
Sleeves are worked side to side.
CO 47 sts and set up patts as follows:
Row 1 (RS): Work 43 sts of Cable
Pattern (Row 1 of chart, between C and
B), p3, work selvage st.
Work Rows 1–104 of chart once, then
Rows 25–108 once (188 rows total).
At the same time, CO 4 sts at end of
2nd row (WS), then every other row 35
times.
Work new sts into patt as soon as you
have enough sts, following chart.
On Row 70, after the last increase,
patts should be set as follows:
Work selvage st, p6, 141 sts in Cable
Pattern (see chart), 38 sts in Cable
Pattern (between D and A), p3, work
selvage st—187 sts.
Work 48 rows in patts as set without
shaping.
BO 4 sts at beg of next row (RS) then
every other row 35 times.
When 188 rows are complete, BO rem
47 sts.

Make 2nd sleeve the same way.

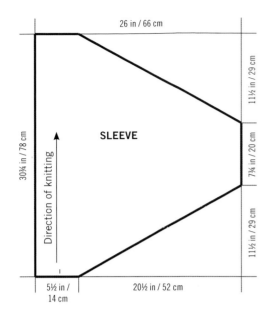

SLEEVE

26 in / 66 cm

30¾ in / 78 cm

Direction of knitting

11½ in / 29 cm

7¾ in / 20 cm

11½ in / 29 cm

5½ in / 14 cm

20½ in / 52 cm

HOOD

Direction of knitting

3-½ in / 80 cm

12 in / 30 cm

FINISHING

Pin out pieces to dimensions shown on schematic. Dampen and allow to dry. Sew shoulder seams. Sew side seams from bottom for about 3 in / 8 cm. Set sleeves into armholes and sew underarm seams. Fold hood in half and sew sides of piece together for top of hood. Sew hood onto neck opening, beginning at the center front. Weave in ends.

KEY

⊟ P

⊡ K

Sl 10 to cn and hold in *front*, sl 7 to second cn and hold in *back*, k1, k7 from second cn, k10 from first cn

CABLE CHART (over 27 sts)

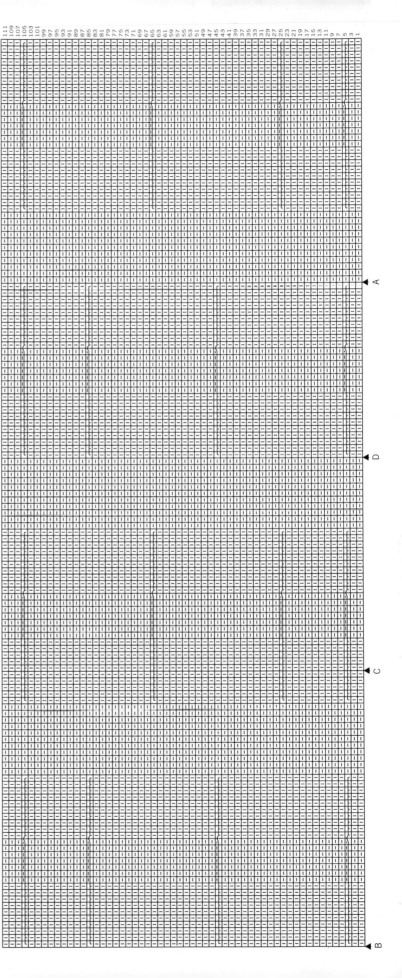

MATERIALS

Yarn:
CYCA #4 (worsted/afghan/aran), Landlust Tweed or equivalent (87 yd/80 m / 50 g)

Yarn Amounts:
#4715 Dark Green, 650 g
#4802 Rust, 350 g
#4847 Dark Turquoise, 350 g

Knitting Needles:
U.S. size 7 and 8 /
4.5 and 5 mm

Crochet Hook:
U.S. size H-8 / 5 mm

Finished Measurements:
Approx. 56 x 36 in / 142 x 92 cm

28 PLAID PONCHO

PATTERN

GAUGE
17 sts and 24 rows in St st = 4 x 4 in / 10 x 10 cm

PATTERN STITCHES
Stockinette Stitch (St st): Knit on RS, purl on WS.
Ribbing: (K1, p1) across.
Checker Pattern (see chart): RS and WS rows are charted.

INSTRUCTIONS
The poncho is made in 2 separate pieces that are sewn together after the knitting is complete.

With Rust and smaller ndls, CO 80 sts. Work in Ribbing for 8 rows. Change to larger ndls and work in Checker Pattern (see chart). Start with 1 row of Dark Turquoise, centering pattern as shown on chart. Work 40-row pattern repeat twice; then work in St st and Dark Green for approx. 26 in / 66 cm (about 160 rows). Then repeat colorwork pattern 2 times, centering the pattern in the same way.
End with 1 row of Dark Turqoise.
Work 8 rows in Rust.
BO.

Make the 2nd piece the same way.

FINISHING

Sew pieces together lengthwise halfway (leaving half unsewn for front opening) with mattress stitch.
On both sides, with smaller needles and Dark Green, pick up and knit 1 st in each st on the edge and work 6 rows in Ribbing. BO.
For the front band, with Dark Green and smaller ndls, CO 8 sts and work in Ribbing for approx. 60 in / 152 cm (about 280 rows). BO. Sew band around front edge with mattress stitch. Wet or steam poncho and dry flat to block.
With Dark Turquoise and crochet hook, work crochet chain onto Checker Pattern, using chart as a guide. (Insert hook through knitting from front to back and pull up a loop. Repeat at even intervals, pulling 2nd loop through first loop on hook to complete each chain.)
Weave in ends.

COLOR CHART

REPEAT (24 STS)

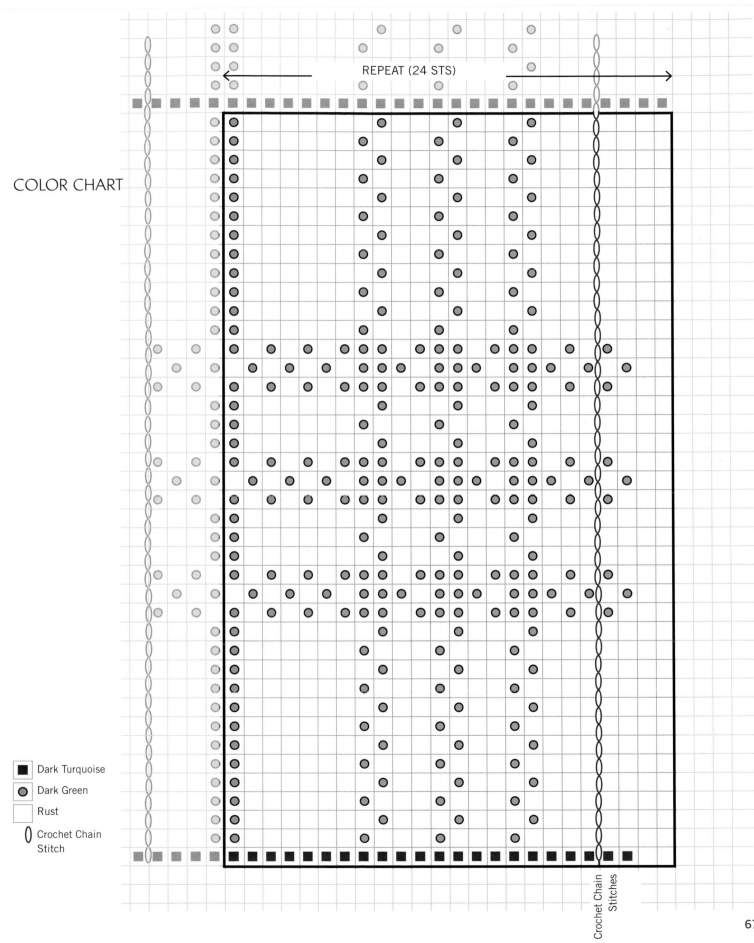

Dark Turquoise

Dark Green

Rust

Crochet Chain
Stitch

Crochet Chain
Stitches

MATERIALS

Yarn:
CYCA #4 (worsted/afghan/
aran), Landlust Tweed or
equivalent (87 yd/80 m /
50 g)

Yarn Amounts:
#4581 Dark Gray, 650 g
#4885 Yellow Green, 750 g
#4805 Turquoise, 850 g

Knitting Needles:
U.S. size 7 and 8 / 4.5 mm
and 5mm and circular
needles U.S. size 7 / 4.6 mm

Size:
S (M, L)

Finished Measurements:
Chest: 42½ (46½, 50½) in /
108 (118, 128) cm

29 FATHER AND SON MEN'S PULLOVER

PATTERN

GAUGE
17 sts and 25 rows in St st with larger
needles = 4 x 4 in / 10 x 10 cm

PATTERN STITCHES
Stockinette Stitch (St st): Knit on RS,
purl on WS.
Color Pattern (see chart): RS and WS
rows are shown.
Ribbing: (K1, p1) across.

DECORATIVE DECREASES
Left-Leaning Decrease: Sl 1 knitwise,
k1, psso.
Right-Leaning Decrease: K2tog.

INSTRUCTIONS
Back
With Medium Gray, CO 92 (102, 112)
sts. Work in Ribbing for 1½ in / 4 cm.
Change to larger ndls.
Work even in St st until piece measures
15½ (15¾, 16¼) in / 39 (40, 41) cm.
Begin Color pattern (see chart),
centering pattern.
Work even until piece measures 16½
(16¾, 17) in / 42 (43, 44) cm.

Armhole Shaping
BO 3 (4, 5) sts at beg of next 2 rows,
then BO 2 sts at beg of next 2 rows.
Then dec beg and end of every other
row 4 (6, 8) times as follows: K2,
k2tog, work to last 4 sts, sl 1, k1, psso,
k2.
Work even until piece measures 26
(26¾, 27½) in / 66 (68, 70) cm.

Neck and Shoulder Shaping
BO center 18 sts; then, working each
shoulder separately, every other row BO
5 sts at neck edge once, then BO 4 sts
at neck edge once. *At the same time,*
every other row at shoulder edge, BO 6
(7, 8) sts twice.
BO rem sts.

Front
With Medium Gray, CO 92 (102, 112)
sts. Work in Ribbing for 1½ in / 4 cm.
Change to larger ndls.
Work even in St st until piece measures
15½ (15¾, 16¼) in / 39 (40, 41) cm.
Begin Color Pattern (see chart), centering
pattern.
Work even until piece measures 16½
(16¾, 17) in / 42 (43, 44) cm.

Armhole Shaping
BO 3 (4, 5) sts at beg of next 2 rows,
then BO 2 sts at beg of next 2 rows. Then
dec beg and end of every other row 4 (6,
8) times as follows: K2; k2tog; work to
last 4 sts; sl 1, k1, psso; k2.
Work even until piece measures 20½
(21½, 22) in / 52 (54, 56) cm.

Neck and Shoulder Shaping
Split into 2 halves and work separately.
Every other row at neck edge, dec 1 st 18
times as follows:
On the left shoulder: K2, k2tog, knit to
end.
On the right shoulder: Knit to last 4 sts; sl
1, k1, psso; k2.
Work even until piece measures 26 (26¾,
27½) in / 66 (68, 70) cm.
Every other row at shoulder edge, BO 6
(7, 8) sts twice.
BO rem sts.

Sleeves
With Medium Gray and smaller ndls, CO
44 (47, 50) sts and work in Ribbing for
1½ in / 4 cm. Change to larger ndls and
St st. Inc beg and end every 6th row 13

times, then every 8th row 3 times—76 (79, 82) sts.

When piece measures approx. 18 in / 46 cm, begin Color Pattern (see chart), centering pattern.

Work even until piece measures 20 in / 51 cm.

Cap Shaping
BO 3 (4, 5) sts at beg of next 2 rows, then BO 2 sts at beg of next 2 rows. Then dec beg and end of every other row 17 times as follows: K2; k2tog; work to last 4 sts; sl 1, k1, psso; k2. Then BO 3 sts at beg of next 2 rows once.

When piece measures 10¼ (10½, 11) in / 26 (27, 28) cm, BO rem 26 (27, 28) sts.

Make 2nd sleeve the same way.

FINISHING

Pin out pieces to dimensions shown on schematic. Dampen and allow to dry. Sew shoulder, side, and underarm seams. Set sleeves into armhole.

Neckband: With smaller ndls, pick up and knit 94 sts around neck (32 sts across back and 62 sts across front) and work in Ribbing for 4 rnds. For the rolled edge, knit 4 rnds. BO.

Weave in ends.

COLOR CHART

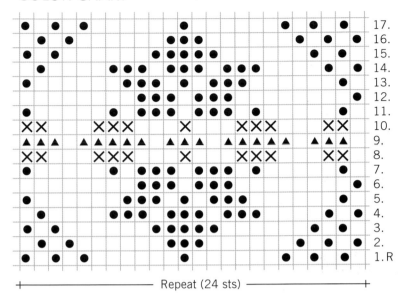

Repeat (24 sts)

Note: Center the pattern on each piece.

- ☐ Medium Gray
- ● Dark Gray
- ✕ Turquoise
- ▲ Yellow Green

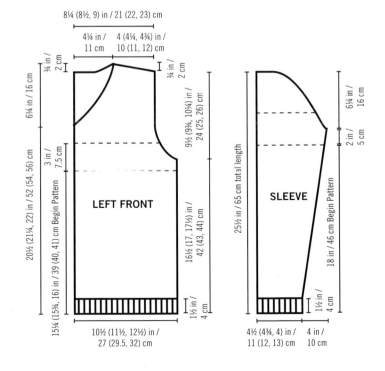

LEFT FRONT

SLEEVE

MATERIALS

Yarn:

CYCA #4 (worsted/afghan/aran), Landlust Tweed or equivalent (87 yd/80 m / 50 g)

Yarn Amounts:

#4596 Natural, 100 g
#2017 Light Gray, 50 g
#4742 Medium Gray, 100 g
#4581 Dark Gray, 50 g
#4898 Petrol, 50 g
#4885 Yellow Green, 50 g
#4805 Turquoise, 50 g

Knitting Needles:

U.S. size 7 and 8 / 4.5 mm and 5mm and circular needle U.S. size 7 / 4.6mm

Size:

Child's size 5

Finished Measurements:

Chest: 26¾ in / 68 cm
Length: approx. 15¾ in / 40 cm

30 FATHER AND SON BOYS' VEST

PATTERN

GAUGE

17 sts and 25 rows in St st with larger needles = 4 x 4 in / 10 x 10 cm

PATTERN STITCHES

Stockinette Stitch (St st): Knit on RS, purl on WS.
Color Patterns 1 and 2 (see Charts A and B): RS and WS rows are shown.
Ribbing: (K1, p1) across.

DECORATIVE DECREASES

Left-Leaning Decrease: Sl 1 knitwise, k1, psso.
Right-Leaning Decrease: K2tog.

Back

With Medium Gray, CO 60 sts. Work in Ribbing for 1¼ in / 3 cm. Change to larger ndls.
Work even in St st until piece measures 4½ in / 11 cm. Begin Color Pattern 1 (see Chart A), centering pattern.
Note: After 9 rows, change background color from Medium Gray to Light Gray. Continue until all rows of Chart A have been completed. Work 2 in / 5 cm in Light Gray.
Begin Color Pattern 2 (see Chart B), centering pattern.
Note: After 11 rows, change background color from Medium Gray to Natural.
Continue until all rows of Chart B have been completed and, *at the same time*, when piece measures 9¾ in / 25 cm, begin armhole shaping as follows.

Armhole Shaping

BO 3 sts at beg of next 2 rows. Then dec beg and end of every other row 5 times as follows: K2; k2tog; work to last 4 sts; sl 1, k1, psso; k2.
Work even until piece measures 15 in / 38 cm.

Neck and Shoulder Shaping

BO center 10 sts; then, working both shoulders *at the same time* with separate balls of yarn, every other row BO 5 sts at neck edge once, then BO 3 sts at neck edge once.
When piece measures 15¾ in / 40 cm, BO rem sts for shoulder.

Front

With Medium Gray, CO 60 sts. Work in Ribbing for 1¼ in / 3 cm. Change to larger ndls.
Work even in St st until piece measures 4½ in / 11 cm. Begin Color Pattern 1 (see Chart A), centering pattern.
Note: After 9 rows, change background color from Medium Gray to Light Gray. Continue until all rows of Chart A have been completed. Work 2 in / 5 cm in Light Gray.
Begin Color Pattern 2 (see Chart B), centering pattern.
Note: After 11 rows, change background color from Medium Gray to Natural.
Continue until all rows of Chart A have been completed and, *at the same time*, when piece measures 9¾ in / 25 cm, begin armhole shaping as follows.

Armhole Shaping

BO 3 sts at beg of next 2 rows. Then dec beg and end of every other row 5 times as follows: K2, k2tog, work to last 4 sts, sl 1, k1, psso, k2.
Work even until piece measures 11½ in / 29 cm.

Neck and Shoulder Shaping

BO center 2 sts, then work the right shoulder first.
Dec every other row at neck edge 12 times as follows k2, ssk, knit to end.

When piece measures 15¾ in / 40 cm,
BO rem sts for shoulder.
On left shoulder, dec every other row at
the neck edge 12 times as follows: knit
to last 4 sts, ssk, k2. When piece
measures 15¾ in / 40 cm, BO rem sts
for shoulder.

FINISHING

Pin out pieces to dimensions shown on
schematic. Dampen and allow to dry.
Sew shoulder and side seams.
Neckband: With smaller ndls, pick up
and knit 32 sts across back neck and
48 sts across front neck. Work in the
round in K1, P1 Ribbing for 3 rnds. For
the rolled edge, knit 3 rnds. BO.
Armbands: With smaller ndls, pick up
and knit 52 sts around armhole. Work
in the round in K1, P1 Ribbing for 8
rnds. BO. Fold the neckband in half to
the inside and stitch in place.
Weave in ends.

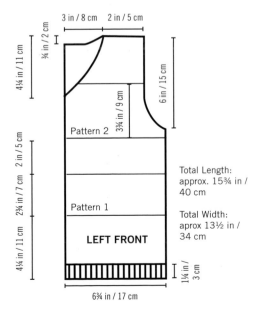

COLOR CHART 1

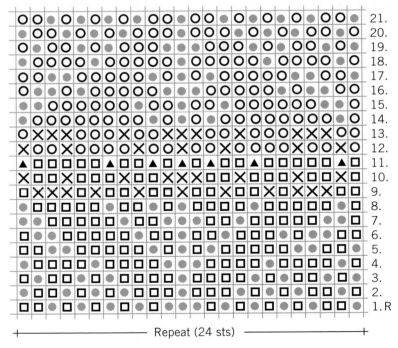

Repeat (24 sts)

☐ Medium Gray
□ Light Gray
● Dark Gray
✕ Turquoise
▲ Yellow Green

Note: Center the pattern on each piece.

COLOR CHART 2

Repeat (24 sts)

□ Light Gray
○ Natural
● Petrol

✕ Turquoise
▲ Yellow Green

DRESSES AND SKIRTS

CHILDREN'S
DRESSES

31 GIRLS' DRESS WITH FAIR ISLE BORDER

32 CHILDREN'S DRESS WITH STRIPES

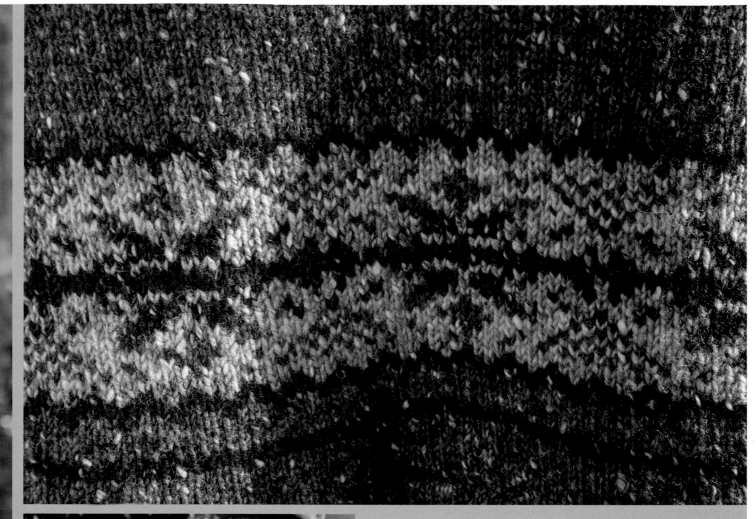

34

FAIR ISLE
BORDER
WOOL SKIRT

MATERIALS

Yarn:
CYCA #4 (worsted/afghan/aran), Landlust Tweed or equivalent (87 yd/80 m / 50 g)

Yarn Amounts:
#4885 Yellow Green, 50 g
#4840 Orange, 50 g
#4816 Fuchsia, 50 g
#4814 Plum, 50 g
#4581 Dark Gray, 50 g
#4596 Natural, 50 g

Knitting Needles:
U.S. size 7 and 8 / 4.5 mm and 5 mm

Crochet Hooks:
U.S. size 7 and H-8 / 4.5 mm and 5 mm

Size:
Child's size 4T-6

Finished Measurements:
Chest: approx. 19½ in / 50 cm
Length: approx. 21¼ / 54 cm

31 GIRLS' DRESS WITH FAIR ISLE BORDER

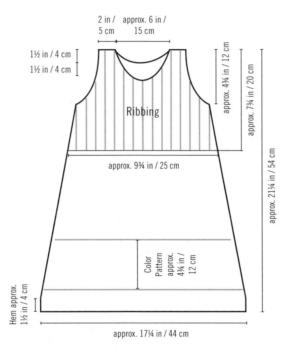

2 in / 5 cm
approx. 6 in / 15 cm
1½ in / 4 cm
1½ in / 4 cm
approx. 4¾ in / 12 cm
approx. 7¾ in / 20 cm
Ribbing
approx. 9¾ in / 25 cm
approx. 21¼ in / 54 cm
Color Pattern approx. 4¾ in / 12 cm
Hem approx. 1½ in / 4 cm
approx. 17¼ in / 44 cm

PATTERN

GAUGE
17 sts and 25 rows in St st with larger needles = 4 x 4 in / 10 x 10 cm

PATTERN STITCHES
Stockinette Stitch (St st): Knit on RS, purl on WS.
Color Pattern (see chart): RS and WS rows are charted.
Ribbing: (K2, p2) across.

DECORATIVE DECREASES
Left-Leaning Decrease: Sl 1 knitwise, k1, psso.
Right-Leaning Decrease: K2tog.

INSTRUCTIONS
Back
With Fuchsia and smaller ndls, CO 74 sts. Work 8 rows in St st.
Work the next row (Row 9) with larger ndls for turning ridge.
Continue with smaller ndls and St st, working stripes as follows:
1 row in Fuchsia
4 rows in Grass Green
2 rows in Plum
4 rows in Grass Green
Begin working Color Pattern (see chart) as follows: Work selvage st, work chart repeat 3 times across, work selvage st.
After all rows of chart are complete, change to Grass Green.
On the 20th row after the turning ridge, begin side shaping as follows:
Decrease row: Work selvage st; sl 1, k1, psso; work patt as set to last 3 sts; k2tog; work selvage st.
Repeat decreases on Row 8 more times, on Rows 30, 40, 50, 58, 66, 74, 82, and 90—9 decrease rows total.
On the 94th row after the turning ridge, 56 sts rem.
Work 10 rows in Ribbing, then begin armhole shaping.

Armhole Shaping
Continue in ribbing and BO 2 sts at beg of next 2 rows.

Dec every RS rows 4 times as follows:
Work 2 sts as set; sl 1, k1, psso; work
to last 4 sts in patt; k2tog; work last 2
sts as set. After all dec rows are
complete, 44 sts rem.
After 36 rows of Ribbing are complete,
begin neck shaping.

Neck Shaping
On the next RS row, BO the center 14
sts. Then, working each side with a
separate ball of yarn, BO 3 sts at neck
edge once, then BO 2 sts at neck edge
once, then BO 1 st at neck edge once.
When piece measures 22 inches (56
cm), BO rem 9 sts at shoulder.

Front
With Fuchsia and smaller ndls, CO 74
sts and work as for back until 24 rows
of ribbing have been completed.

Neck Shaping
On the next RS row, BO the center 10
sts. Then working each side with a
separate ball of yarn, BO 3 sts at neck
edge once, then BO 2 sts at neck edge
once, then work Decorative Decreases
to dec 1 st at neck edge every other
row 3 times. When piece measures 22
inches (56 cm), BO rem 9 sts at
shoulder.

FINISHING

Pin out pieces to dimensions shown on
schematic. Dampen and allow to dry.
Sew side seams and shoulder seams.
Fold the hem up on the front and back
and whip stitch in place.
On the neck and armhole openings,
work 1 round of single crochet with
Orange, then change to Fuchsia and
work 1 round of crab stitch (reverse
single crochet).
Weave in ends.

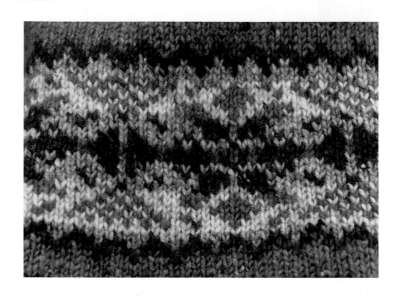

COLOR PATTERN CHART

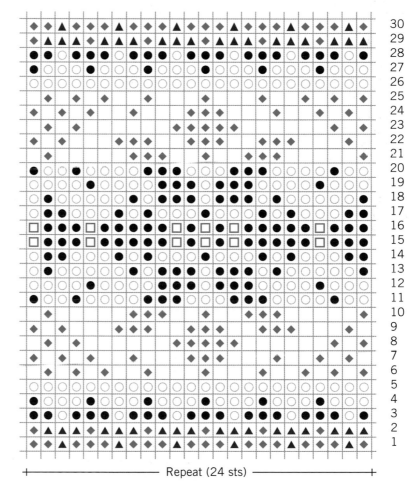

Repeat (24 sts)

▲ Fuchsia   □ Natural
◆ Grass Green   ☐ Orange
● Plum   ○ Dark Gray

MATERIALS

Yarn:
CYCA #4 (worsted/afghan/ aran), Landlust Tweed or equivalent (87 yd/80 m / 50 g)

Yarn Amounts:
#4824 Grass Green, 200 g
#4840 Orange, 50 g
#4816 Fuchsia, 50 g
#4814 Plum, 50 g
#2017 Light Gray, 50 g
#4596 Natural, 50 g

Knitting Needles:
U.S. size 7 and 8 / 4.5 mm and 5 mm

Crochet Hooks:
U.S. size 7 and H-8 / 4.5 mm and 5 mm

Size:
Child's size 4T-6

32 GIRLS' DRESS WITH STRIPES

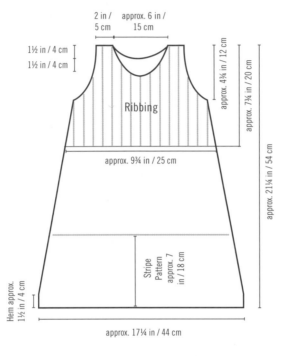

PATTERN

GAUGE
17 sts and 25 rows in St st with larger needles = 4 x 4 in / 10 x 10 cm

PATTERN STITCHES
Stockinette Stitch (St st): Knit on RS, purl on WS.
Stripe Pattern (see diagram): RS and WS rows are listed.
Ribbing: (K2, p2) across.

DECORATIVE DECREASES
Left-Leaning Decrease: Sl 1 knitwise, k1, psso.
Right-Leaning Decrease: K2tog.

INSTRUCTIONS
Back
With Plum and smaller ndls, CO 74 sts. Work 8 rows in St st.
Work the next row (Row 9) with Orange and larger ndls for turning ridge. Continue with smaller ndls and St st and work 5 more rows in Orange (6 rows of Orange total).
Continue working Stripe Pattern (see diagram).
After all stripes are complete, change to Grass Green.
On the 20th row after the turning ridge, begin side shaping as follows:
Decrease row: Work selvage st; sl 1, k1, psso; work patt as set to last 3 sts; k2tog; work selvage st.
Repeat decreases on Row 8 more times, on Rows 30, 40, 50, 58, 66, 74, 82, and 90—9 decrease rows total.
On the 94th row after the turning ridge, 56 sts rem.
Work 10 rows in Ribbing, then begin armhole shaping.

Armhole Shaping
Continue in Ribbing and BO 2 sts at beg of next 2 rows.
Dec every RS rows 4 times as follows: Work 2 sts as set; sl 1, k1, psso; work to last 4 sts in patt; k2tog; work last 2 sts as set. After all dec rows are complete, 44 sts rem.
After 36 rows of Ribbing are complete, begin neck shaping.

Neck Shaping
On the next RS row, BO the center 14 sts. Then, working each side with a separate ball of yarn, BO 3 sts at neck edge once, then BO 2 sts at neck edge

once, then BO 1 st at neck edge once.
When piece measures 22 inches (56 cm),
BO rem 9 sts at shoulder.

Front
With Plum and smaller ndls, CO 74 sts and
work as for back until 24 rows of ribbing
have been completed.

Neck Shaping
On the next RS row, BO the center 10 sts.
Then, working each side with a separate
ball of yarn, BO 3 sts at neck edge once,
then BO 2 sts at neck edge once, then work
Decorative Decreases to dec 1 st at neck
edge every other row 3 times. When piece
measures 22 inches (56 cm), BO rem 9 sts
at shoulder.

FINISHING

Pin out pieces to dimensions shown on
schematic. Dampen and allow to dry.
Sew side seams and shoulder seams. Fold
the hem up on the front and back and whip
stitch in place.
On the neck and armhole openings, work 1
round of single crochet with Orange, then
change to Fuchsia and work 1 round of
crab stitch (reverse single crochet).
Weave in ends.

STRIPE PATTERN DIAGRAM

2 rows Fuchsia
2 rows Orange
2 rows Natural
4 rows Plum
6 rows Grass Green
2 rows Light Gray
4 rows Fuchsia
4 rows Orange
2 rows Natural
2 rows Plum
2 rows Grass Green
2 rows Light Gray
4 rows Fuchsia
6 rows Orange
8 rows Plum (hem)

MATERIALS

Yarn:
CYCA #4 (worsted/afghan/
aran), Landlust Tweed
or equivalent
(87 yd/80 m / 50 g)

Yarn Amounts:
#4898 Petrol Blue,
800 (900) g

Knitting Needles:
U.S. sizes 8, 9, and 11 / 5,
5.5, and 8 mm needles

U.S. size 8 / 5 mm circular
needle for neck

Notions:
Two fabric pieces, approx.
7–8 in / 18–20 cm wide for
the pockets

Size:
S (M/L) When only one
number is given, it applies
to both sizes.

Finished Measurements:
Bust: 44 (47¼) in / 112
(120) cm
Length: 38½ (40) in / 98
(102) cm

33 COZY FELTED DRESS

PATTERN

GAUGE
16 sts and 23 rows in St st with U.S.
size 9 / 5.5 mm needles = 4 x 4 in /
10 x 10 cm

PATTERN STITCHES
Stockinette Stitch (St st): Knit RS rows,
purl WS rows.
Ribbing: (K2, p2) across.

DECORATIVE DECREASES
At the beginning of the row, work 2 sts,
then k3tog (right-slanting double

decrease), then continue in patt.
At the end of the row, work to the last 5
sts, then sl 1 knitwise, k2tog, psso
(left-slanting double decrease), then work
last 2 sts.

INSTRUCTIONS
Back
With smallest ndls, CO 90 (98) sts. Work
8 rows in Ribbing, then change to
medium ndl and St st.
When piece measures 4¾ inches (12
cm), on the next RS row begin side
increases as follows:
Inc row: Work 3 sts in patt, M1, work to
last 3 sts, M1, work to end of row—92
(100) sts.
Inc at beg and end of row in this manner
every 10th row 3 times then on the 20th
row once—100 (108) sts.
Cont in St st without increasing.
When piece measures 22 inches (56
cm), on the next RS row begin side
decreases as follows:
Dec row: Work 2 sts in patt; k3tog; work
to last 5 sts in patt; sl 1, k2tog, psso;
work last 2 sts in patt.
Dec at beg and end of row in this manner
every 10th row 3 more times—84 (92)
sts.
Cont in St st without decreasing.

When piece measures approx. 29½ (30)
inches / 75 (77) cm, about 14 rows after
the last decrease row, CO 4 sts at beg of
next 2 rows—92 (100) sts.
Work even in St st.

When piece measures approx. 37 (38½)
inches / 94 (98) cm, begin shoulder
shaping as follows: BO 4 sts at beg of
next 2 rows 5 times.

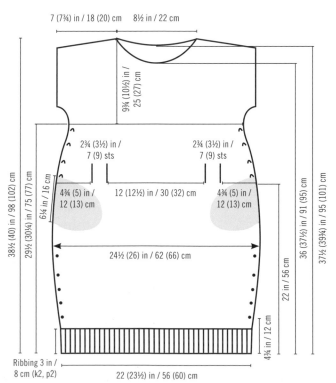

7 (7¾) in / 18 (20) cm   8½ in / 22 cm

9¾ (10½) in /
25 (27) cm

2¾ (3½) in /
7 (9) sts

2¾ (3½) in /
7 (9) sts

4¾ (5) in /
12 (13) cm

12 (12½) in / 30 (32) cm

4¾ (5) in /
12 (13) cm

38½ (40) in / 98 (102) cm

29½ (30¼) in / 75 (77) cm

6¾ in / 16 cm

24½ (26) in / 62 (66) cm

36 (37½) in / 91 (95) cm

37½ (39¾) in / 95 (101) cm

22 in / 56 cm

4¾ in / 12 cm

Ribbing 3 in /
8 cm (k2, p2)

22 (23½) in / 56 (60) cm

?????

Missing text

84

Tip for experts: Work shoulder shaping with short rows.

At the same time, when piece measures approx. 37¼ (38¾) inches / 95 (99) cm, begin neck shaping as follows:
On the next row, put the center 20 sts on hold. Then, working each side with a separate ball of yarn, at the neck edge every other row put 4 more sts on hold once then put 2 sts on hold twice.
Tip: Use the wrap and turn technique when leaving stitches unworked. To avoid holes when you pick up stitches later for the neckband, pick up the wrap along with the wrapped stitch.

When piece measures approx. 38½ (40) inches / 98 (102) cm, BO rem sts at shoulders Put the neck stitches on hold on circular ndl.

Front

With smallest ndls, CO 90 (98) sts.
Work 8 rows in Ribbing, then change to medium ndl and St st.
When piece measures 4¾ inches (12 cm), on the next RS row begin side increases as follows (see schematic):
Inc row: Work 3 sts in patt, M1, work to last 3 sts, M1, work to end of row—92 (100) sts.
Inc at beg and end of row in this manner every 10th row 3 times then on the 20th row once—100 (108) sts.
Cont in St st without increasing.
When piece measures 22 inches (56 cm), on the next RS row begin side decreases as follows:
Dec row: Work 2 sts in patt; k3tog; work to last 5 sts in patt; sl 1, k2tog, psso; work last 2 sts in patt.
Dec at beg and end of row in this manner every 10th row 3 more times—84 (92) sts.
Cont in St st without decreasing.

When piece measures approx. 29½ (30) inches / 75 (77) cm, about 14 rows after the last decrease row, CO 4 sts at beg of next 2 rows—92 (100) sts.
Work even in St st.

When piece measures approx. 36 (37½) inches / 91 (95) cm, begin neck shaping as follows:
On the next row, put the center 12 sts on hold. Then, working each side with

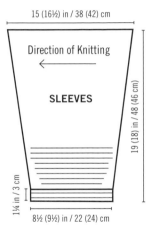

15 (16½) in / 38 (42) cm

Direction of Knitting

SLEEVES

19 (18) in / 48 (46) cm

1¼ in / 3 cm

8½ (9½) in / 22 (24) cm

a separate ball of yarn, at the neck edge every other row put 5 more sts on hold once, then put 3 sts on hold once, then put 2 sts on hold twice, then put 1 st on hold twice (see back instructions for tip).

When piece measures approx. 37 (38½) inches / 94 (98) cm, begin shoulder shaping as follows: BO 4 sts at beg of next 2 rows 5 times.
Tip for experts: Work shoulder shaping with short rows.

When piece measures approx. 38½ (40) inches / 98 (102) cm, BO rem sts at shoulders Put the neck stitches on hold on circular ndl.

Sleeves
(worked side to side)
With medum ndls, CO 4 sts and purl 1 row.
Begin increasing as follows:
Next row (RS): Knit across, CO 2 sts.
Next row (WS): Purl.
Continue in this fashion and at the end of RS rows CO 6 sts once, then 8 sts once, then 10 sts once, then 12 sts once, then 14 sts once, then 22 (16) sts once—78 (72) sts.
Next row (WS): Work selvage st, p4, k1 (turning ridge), p71 (65), work selvage st.
Next row (RS): Work sts as they appear (knit the knits and purl the purls).
Work even in patt as set until piece measures approx. 8½ (9½) inches / 22 (24) cm at the cuff edge.
Then reverse shaping as follows:
Next row (WS): BO 22 (16) sts, purl to end.

Next row (RS): Knit.
Continue in this fashion and at the beginning of WS rows BO 14 sts once, then 12 sts once, then 10 sts once, then 8 sts once, then 6 sts once, then 2 sts once.
BO rem 4 sts.

Collar
On the held back-neck sts, with the medium ndls, work approx. 1 inch / 3 cm of St st. For turning ridge, work 1 row with largest ndls. With medium ndls, work another 1 inch / 3 cm of St st. BO.
Repeat on held front-neck sts.

FINISHING

Pin out pieces to dimensions shown on schematic.
Turn collar on front and back to inside on fold line and sew in place.
Fold cuff to inside on fold line and sew in place.
Sew side seams and shoulder seams, leaving openings for pockets (see schematic).
Make pocket inserts from fabric and sew into pocket openings.
Weave in ends.

Create darts in the front as follows (see schematic): Approx. 4¾ (5) in / 12 (13) cm from side edges, fold 7 (9) stitches together. Use mattress stitch on the RS to sew the fold in place.

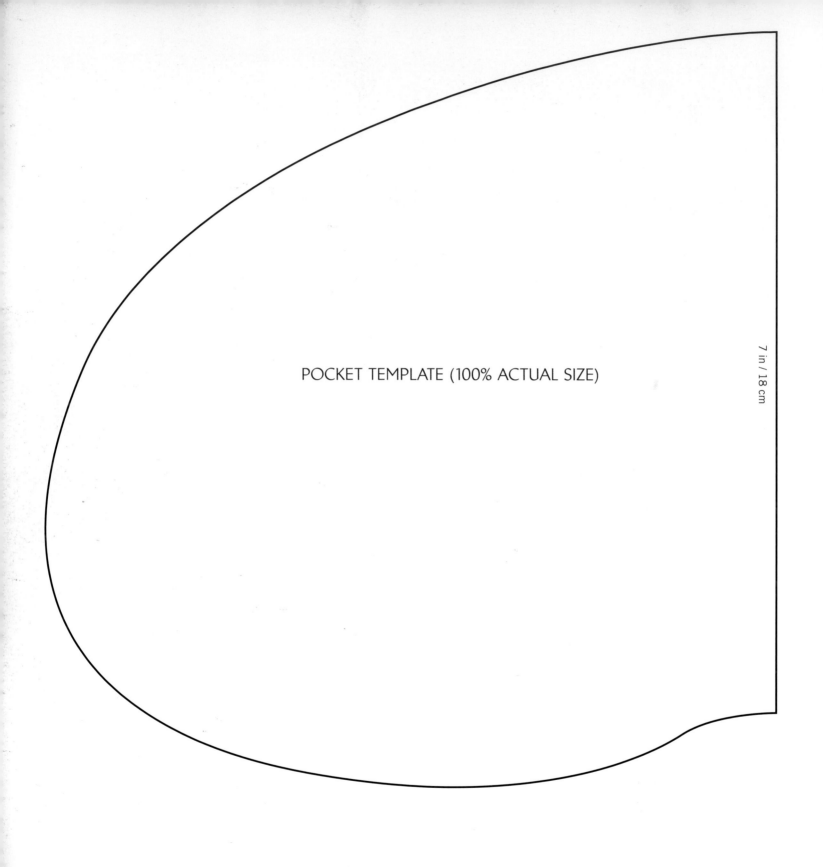

POCKET TEMPLATE (100% ACTUAL SIZE)

7 in / 18 cm

MATERIALS

Size:
S (M)

Yarn:
CYCA #4 (worsted/afghan/aran), Landlust Tweed or equivalent (87 yd/80 m / 50 g)

Yarn Amounts:
#4582 Stone Gray, 400 (500) g
#4754 Landlust Red, 50 g
#4581 Dark Gray, 50 g
#4742 Medium Gray, 50 g
#2017 Light Gray, 50 g

Knitting Needles:
U.S. sizes 6 and 8 / 4 and 5 mm

Notions:
Elastic for waistband

Size:
S (M)

Finished Measurements:
Waist: 26½ (27½) in / 34 (35) cm
Length: 23½ in / 60 cm

34 FAIR ISLE BORDER WOOL SKIRT

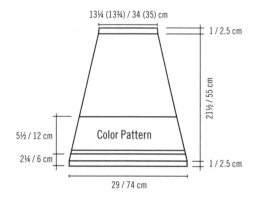

PATTERN

GAUGE
17 sts and 25 rnds in St st with larger needles = 4 x 4 in / 10 x 10 cm

PATTERN STITCHES
Stockinette Stitch (St st): Knit all rnds.
Color Pattern: see chart.

DECORATIVE DECREASES
Left-Leaning Decrease: Sl 1 knitwise, k1, psso.
Right-Leaning Decrease: K2tog.

INSTRUCTIONS
With Stone Gray and smaller ndl, CO 252 sts. Join to work in the round, being careful not to twist. Work in St st as follows:
Rnds 1–7: Work in Stone Gray.

Rnd 8: Work in Landlust Red.
Rnd 9: Change to larger ndl and work in Landlust Red for turning ridge.
Rnd 10: Change to smaller ndl and work in Landlust Red.
Rnds 11–18: Work in Stone Gray.
Rnds 19–27: Change to larger ndl and work in Stone Gray.
On the next rnd, divide sts into 3 equal sections with markers.
Rnd 28 (dec rnd): *Slip marker, k1; sl 1, k1, psso; work to last 3 sts before next marker, k2tog, k1; rep from * two more times.
Rnds 29–30: Work in Dark Gray.
Rnds 31–33: Work in Stone Gray.
Rnd 34: Rep Rnd 28—240 sts rem.
Begin Color Pattern (see chart). Center the pattern and work the 24-stitch repeat 10 times around.
After completing all rows of the chart, continue in Stone Gray; decrease as above every 6th rnd 5 (20) times, then every 4th rnd 15 (0) times—120 (150) sts rem.

When piece measures 22½ in / 57 cm from foldline, work waistband as follows:
With smaller ndl and Stone Gray, work 8 rnds of St st. Work the next rnd with larger ndls for turning ridge, then work 8 more rnds with smaller ndl.
BO all sts.

COLOR CHART

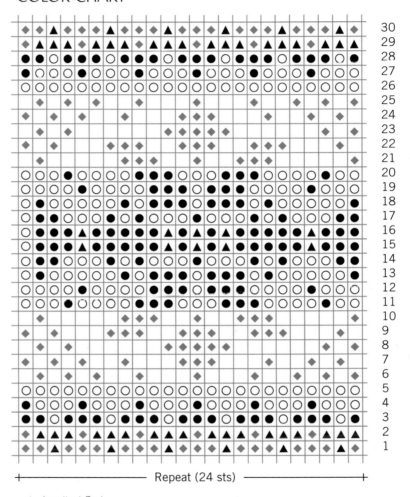

Repeat (24 sts)

FINISHING

Fold the hem up and stitch in place.
Fold the waistband down and stitch in place, leaving a small opening to insert elastic.
Weave in cnds.

▲ Landlust Red
◆ Stone Gray
● Dark Gray
☐ Light Gray
○ Medium Gray

AT HOME OR ON THE GO

35

36

37

38

39

LITTLE
PILLOW
PARADE

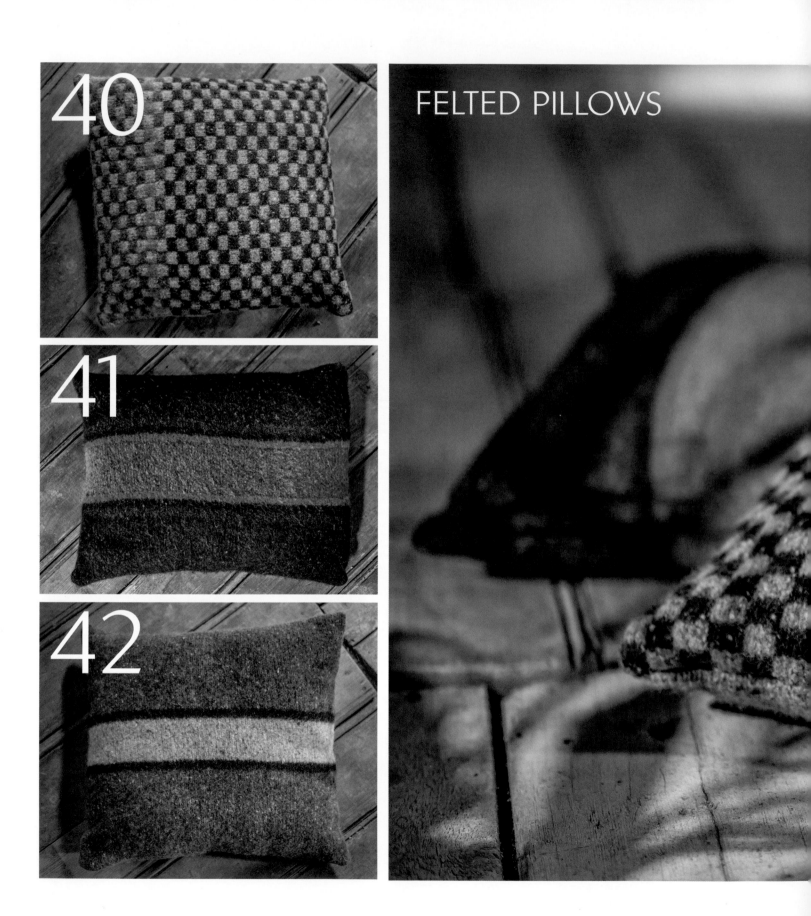

40

41

42

FELTED PILLOWS

43
BUM WARMER
SEAT PADS

44 FELTED
SHOULDER BAG

45
FELTED
SHOPPING BAG

46

LITTLE
COMPANION

47
HAIRPIN LACE AFGHAN

48

49

ROUND FLOOR
CUSHIONS

51

52 BICYCLE SEAT COVERS

MATERIALS

DARK GREEN CUSHION

Yarn:
CYCA #4 (worsted/afghan/aran), Landlust Tweed or equivalent (87 yd/80 m / 50 g)

Yarn Amounts:
#4715 Dark Green, 100 g

Knitting Needles:
U.S. size 8 / 5 mm

Finished Measurements:
Approx. 16 x 16 in / 40 x 40 cm

GRASS GREEN CUSHION

Yarn:
CYCA #4 (worsted/afghan/aran), Landlust Tweed or equivalent (87 yd/80 m / 50 g)

Yarn Amounts:
#4824 Grass Green, 100 g

Knitting Needles:
U.S. size 8 / 5 mm

Notions:
Fabric for backing pillows, approx. 17 x 17 in / 43 x 43 cm, pillow form 16 x 16 in / 40 x 40 cm, sewing needle and matching thread.

Finished Measurements:
Approx. 15¾ x 15¾ in / 40 x 40 cm

FINISHING

FOR CUSHIONS 35–39

Cut yarn. Use the knitted piece for the cushion front and fabric for the back. Fold a seam allowance in on the fabric so the fabric piece is the same size as the knitting. Place the two pieces with WS together, and use the needle and thread sew the knitting to the fabric leaving an opening to insert the pillow form. After inserting the pillow form, stitch the opening closed.

35/36/37/38 LITTLE PILLOW PARADE

DARK GREEN CUSHION

GAUGE
17 sts and 23 rows in St st = 4 x 4 in / 10 x 10 cm

PATTERN STITCHES
Stockinette Stitch (St st): Knit on RS, purl on WS.
Reverse Stockinette Stitch (rev St st): Purl on RS, knit on WS.

INSTRUCTIONS
CO 68 sts. *Work 8 rows of St st, then 8 rows of rev St st; rep from * 5 more times or until piece measures approx. 16 in / 40 cm. End after a purl section. BO.

FINISHING

See instructions on left.

GRASS GREEN CUSHION

GAUGE
17 sts and 23 rows in St st = 4 x 4 in / 10 x 10 cm

PATTERN STITCH
Ribbing: (K2, p2) across. Work as set for 4 rows.
The pattern shifts 1 st to the left every 4 rows to form diagonal lines.

INSTRUCTIONS
CO 68 sts.
Row 1: (P2, k2) across.
Rows 2–4: Work Ribbing as set.
Row 5: K1, (p2, k2) to last 3 sts, p2, k1.
Rows 6–8: Work Ribbing as set.
Row 9: (K2, p2) across.
Rows 10–12: Work Ribbing as set.
Row 13: P1, (k2, p2) to last 3 sts, k2, p1.
Rows 14–16: Work Ribbing as set.
Rep Rows 1–16 until piece measures approx. 16 in / 40 cm.
BO.

FINISHING

See instructions on left.

DARK BROWN CUSHION

GAUGE
17 sts and 23 rows in St st = 4 x 4 in / 10 x 10 cm

PATTERN STITCH
Row 1: (K7, p7) across.
Row 2: Work sts as they appear (knit the knits, purl the purls).
Pattern shifts 1 st to the left after ever 2 rows.

INSTRUCTIONS
CO 70 sts.
Row 1: (K7, p7) across.
Row 2 (and all WS rows): Work sts as they appear.
Row 3: K6, (p7, k7) to last 8 sts, p7, k1.
Row 5: K5, (p7, k7) to last 9 sts, p7, k2.
Row 7: K4, (p7, k7) to last 9 sts, p7, k3.
Continue in this fashion, shifting the pattern to the left 1 st on every RS row. Work in patt until piece measures approx. 16 in / 40 cm.
BO.

Flower
With dpn, CO 40 sts. Divide sts into 4 equal sections of 10 sts each on 4 dpn. Join to work in the round, being careful not to twist.
Rnd 1: Knit.
Rnd 2: *K2, yo, k2, yo; rep from * around.
Rnd 3: Knit.
Rnd 4: *K2, yo, k2, yo; rep from * around.
Rnd 5: Knit.
Continue in this fashion until flower is desired size. (If you work more than 11 rnds, you may need to switch to a circular.)

Knit 2 rnds with no increases.
BO.

FINISHING

Thread CO tail of flower onto a tapestry needle; weave yarn through CO sts and gather together. Sew flower onto pillow front. Weave in ends.
See instructions on left.

STRIPED CUSHION

GAUGE
17 sts and 23 rows in St st = 4 x 4 in / 10 x 10 cm

PATTERN STITCHES
Ribbing: (K4, p4) across, changing colors after every 4 rows for stripes.

INSTRUCTIONS
With Natural, CO 74 sts.
Rows 1 and 2: Work selvage st, (p4, k4) 9 times, work selvage st.
Rows 3 and 4: Selvage st, work sts as they appear to last st, work selvage st. Change to Dark Brown.
Rows 5 and 7: Work selvage st, (k4, p4) 9 times, work selvage st.
Rows 6 and 8: Work as Row 2.
Rows 9–12: Change to Fuchsia. Rep Rows 1–4.
Rows 13–16: Change to Petrol. Rep Rows 2–8
Rep Rows 1–16 until piece measures approx. 16 in / 40 cm.
BO.

FINISHING

Work 1 row of sc around edge of piece. Weave in ends.
See instructions on left.

MATERIALS

DARK BROWN CUSHION
Yarn:
CYCA #4 (worsted/afghan/aran), Landlust Tweed or equivalent (87 yd/80 m / 50 g)

Yarn Amounts:
#4741 Dark Brown, 100 g

Knitting Needles:
U.S. size 8 / 5 mm straight or circular needles, and set of 5 dpn for flower

Notions:
Fabric for backing pillows, approx. 17 x 17 in / 43 x 43 cm, pillow form 16 x 16 in / 40 x 40 cm, sewing needle and matching thread.

Finished Measurements:
Approx. 15¾ x 15¾ in / 40 x 40 cm

STRIPED CUSHION
Yarn:
CYCA #4 (worsted/afghan/aran), Landlust Tweed or equivalent (87 yd/80 m / 50 g)

Yarn Amounts:
Total approx. 80 g in 5 colors:
#4596 Natural
#4741 Dark Brown
#4816 Fuchsia
#4898 Petrol
#4843 Blackberry

Knitting Needles:
U.S. size 8 / 5 mm

Notions:
Fabric for backing pillows, approx. 17 x 17 in / 43 x 43 cm, pillow form 16 x 16 in / 40 x 40 cm, sewing needle and matching thread.

Finished Measurements:
Approx. 15¾ x 15¾ in / 40 x 40 cm

MATERIALS

LIGHT GRAY PILLOW

Yarn:
CYCA #4 (worsted/afghan/aran), Landlust Tweed or equivalent (87 yd/80 m / 50 g), 100 g in #2017 Light Gray

Knitting Needles:
U.S. size 6 / 4 mm circular and set of 5 dpn

Notions:
Fabric for backing pillows, approx. 17 x 17 in / 43 x 43 cm, pillow form 16 x 16 in / 40 x 40 cm, sewing needle and matching thread.

Finished Measurements:
Approx. 15¾ x 15¾ in / 40 x 40 cm

GAUGE

17 sts and 23 rows in St st = 4 x 4 in / 10 x 10 cm

PATTERN STITCH

Stockinette Stitch (St st): Knit on RS, purl on WS.

39 LITTLE PILLOW PARADE

LIGHT GRAY PILLOW

INSTRUCTIONS

With dpns, CO 20 sts. Divide sts evenly onto 4 ndls (5 sts per ndl). Join to work in the round, being careful not to twist.
Rnd 1: Knit.
Rnd 2: *K2, m1 (insert left ndl under bar between sts from front to back, knit this through the back), k1 (middle st on the ndl), m1, k2; rep from * on next 3 ndls (7 sts on each ndl).
Rnd 3: Knit (without increasing).
Rnd 4: *K3, m1, k1 (middle st on ndl), m1, k3; rep from * on next 3 ndls (9 sts on each ndl).
Rnd 5: Knit (without increasing).
Continue in this fashion and inc 2 sts (1 st before and 1 st after center st on each ndl) every other rnd until piece measures approx. 15¾ x 15¾ in / 40 x 40 cm. (**Tip:** Switch to circular ndl when sts no longer fit comfortably on dpns.)
BO.

Flower

With dpns, CO 60 sts. Divide sts evenly onto 4 ndls (15 sts each ndl). Join to work in the round, being careful not to twist.
Rnd 1: Knit.
Rnd 2: *K2, yo, k2, yo; rep from * around.
Rnd 3: Knit.
Rnd 4: *K2, yo, k2, yo; rep from * around.
Rnd 5: Knit.
Continue in this fashion until flower is desired size. (If you work more than 11 rnds, you may need to switch to a circular.)
Knit 2 rnds with no increases.
BO.

FINISHING

Thread CO tail of flower onto a tapestry needle; weave yarn through CO sts and gather together. Sew flower onto pillow front. Weave in ends.
See instructions on page 106.

40 FELTED CHECK PILLOW

PATTERN

GAUGE
15 sts and 20 rows in St st = 4 x 4 in / 10 x 10 cm before felting

PATTERN STITCHES
Stockinette Stitch (St st): Knit on RS, purl on WS
Check Pattern: See chart.

Note: This pillow is made with knitted pieces for both the front and the back, because the felting process is not exact. If the first piece felts smaller than desired, make the second piece larger at the seam allowance.

INSTRUCTIONS

Front
With Light Gray, CO 82 sts. Work in Check Pattern (see chart) with Light Gray and Dark Gray until 72 rows have been completed. Then change colors as follows:
Work 4 rows with Dark Gray and Yellow Green.
Work 4 rows with Light Gray and Stone Gray.
Work 4 rows in Light Gray and Dark Turquoise.
BO.

Back
With Light Gray, CO 82 sts and work in St st for 110 rows.
BO.

FINISHING

Felt the pieces using hot water and the normal cycle in the washing machine. (**Note:** The exact size after felting may be different in different washing machines. If the pieces are too big, try tumble drying them to shrink them more.)

Stretch the pieces to approx. 15¾ x 15¾ in / 40 x 40 cm and allow to dry thoroughly. Sew the two pieces together, leaving an opening to insert the pillow form. Sew the opening closed after inserting the pillow form. (**Tip:** Sew the opening closed with cotton thread so it can be easily opened again to remove the pillow form for washing.)

MATERIALS

Yarn:
CYCA #4 (worsted/afghan/aran), Landlust Tweed or equivalent (87 yd/80 m / 50 g)

Yarn Amounts:
Total approx. 500 g in 5 colors:
#2017 Light Gray, 250 g
#4581 Dark Gray, 100 g
50 g each of:
#4582 Stone Gray
#4847 Dark Turquoise
#4885 Yellow Green

Knitting Needles:
U.S. size 10 / 6 mm

Notions:
Pillow form 16 x 16 in / 40 x 40 cm, cotton thread and sewing needle

Finished Measurements:
Before felting: Approx. 21 x 23½ in / 54 x 60 cm
After felting: Approx. 15¾ x 15¾ in / 40 x 40 cm

CHECK PATTERN CHART

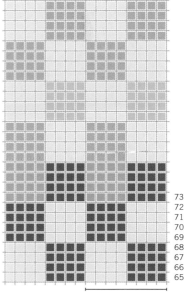

73
72
71
70
69
68
67
66
65

Repeat (8 sts and 8 rows)

☐ Light Gray
▨ Stone Gray
■ Dark Gray
▦ Dark Turquoise
▩ Yellow Green

41/42 STRIPED FELTED PILLOWS

MATERIALS

LANDLUST RED AND GRAY PILLOW

Yarn:
CYCA #4 (worsted/afghan/aran), Landlust Tweed or equivalent (87 yd/80 m / 50 g)

Yarn Amounts:
#4741 Dark Brown, 200 g
#4582 Stone Gray, 100 g
#2017 Light Gray, 50 g
#4754 Landlust Red, 50 g

Knitting Needles:
U.S. size 10 / 6 mm

Notions:
Pillow form 16 x 16 in / 40 x 40 cm, cotton thread and sewing needle

Finished Measurements:
Before felting: Approx. 21 x 47 in / 54 x 120 cm
After felting and sewing: Approx. 15¾ x 15¾ in / 40 x 40 cm

ORANGE AND GREEN PILLOW

Yarn:
CYCA #4 (worsted/afghan/aran), Landlust Tweed or equivalent (87 yd/80 m / 50 g)

Yarn Amounts:
#4843 Blackberry, 300 g
#4824 Grass Green, 100 g
#4814 Plum, 50 g
#4840 Orange, 50 g

Knitting Needles:
U.S. size 10 / 6 mm

Notions:
Pillow form 16 x 8 in / 40 x 20 cm, cotton thread and sewing needle

Finished Measurements:
Before felting: Approx. 21¼ x 23½ in / 54 x 60 cm
After felting: Approx. 15¾ x 8 in / 40 x 20 cm

LANDLUST RED FELTED PILLOW

GAUGE
15 sts and 20 rows in St st = 4 x 4 in / 10 x 10 cm before felting

PATTERN STITCHES
Stockinette Stitch (St st): Knit on RS, purl on WS

INSTRUCTIONS
With Dark Brown, CO 80 sts. Work in St st, changing colors for stripes as follows:
32 rows Dark Brown
14 rows Stone Gray
4 rows Landlust Red
20 rows Light Gray
4 rows Landlust Red
14 rows Stone Gray
64 rows Dark Brown
14 rows Stone Gray
4 rows Landlust Red
20 rows Light Gray
4 rows Landlust Red
14 rows Stone Gray
32 rows Dark Brown
BO.

FINISHING

FOR BOTH PILLOWS
Felt the pieces using hot water and the normal cycle in the washing machine. (**Note:** The exact size after felting may be different in different washing machines. If the pieces are too big, try tumble drying them to shrink them more.)

ORANGE AND GREEN FELTED PILLOW

GAUGE
15 sts and 20 rows in St st = 4 x 4 in / 10 x 10 cm before felting

PATTERN STITCHES
Stockinette Stitch (St st): Knit on RS, purl on WS

INSTRUCTIONS
With Blackberry, CO 90 sts.

Front
Work in St st, changing colors for stripes as follows:
40 rows in Blackberry
6 rows in Plum
4 rows in Blackberry
4 rows in Orange
30 rows in Grass Green
4 rows in Orange
4 rows in Blackberry
6 rows in Plum
40 rows in Blackberry

Back
Repeat the 138-row stripe pattern.
BO.

Stretch the pieces to match size of pillow form and allow to dry thoroughly. Sew the two pieces together, leaving an opening to insert the pillow form. Sew the opening closed after inserting the pillow form.

43 WARM SEAT PADS

PATTERN

INSTRUCTIONS

Ch 8 with any color. Join with sl st to form a ring. Work into ring as follows:

Rnd 1: Work 12 sc in ring. (**Tip:** Mark the beginning of the round with a length of contrasting color yarn.)

Rnd 2: (Sc in next sc, 2 sc in next sc) around.

Rnd 3: (Sc in next 2 sc, 2 sc in next sc) around.

Continue in this fashion, with 1 more sc before each inc in every rnd, changing colors at will. After 28 rnds are finished, fasten off.

FINISHING

Weave in ends.

TIPS

To avoid the piece becoming a hexagon, work Rnd 10 as follows: 5 sc, (2 sc in next sc, sc in next 10 sc) around, ending with 5 sc.

For a ruffled edge, on Rnd 27, work 2 sc in each sc, then on rnd 28 sc in each sc with no increases.

If you prefer to work circular rounds instead of spirals, join each rnd with a sl st and begin each rnd with 1 turning ch.

MATERIALS

Yarn:
CYCA #4 (worsted/afghan/aran), Landlust Tweed or equivalent (87 yd/80 m / 50 g)

Yarn Amounts:
Total (for each cushion), approx. 80 g in various colors of your choice

Crochet Hook:
U.S. size G-6 / 4 mm

Notions:
Tapestry needle

Finished Measurements:
Circumference: approx. 13¾ in / 35 cm

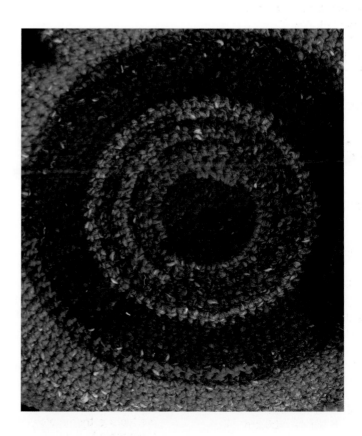

MATERIALS

Yarn:
CYCA #4 (worsted/afghan/ aran), Landlust Tweed or equivalent (87 yd/80 m / 50 g)

Yarn Amounts:
#4741 Dark Brown, 450 g
#4843 Blackberry, 100 g
#4814 Plum, 50 g
#4816 Fuchsia, 50 g

Knitting Needles:
U.S. size 10 / 6 mm circular and straight needles

Finished Measurements:
Circumference: approx. 11 in / 28 cm, before felting

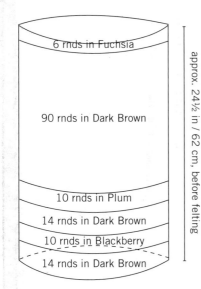

6 rnds in Fuchsia

90 rnds in Dark Brown

approx. 24½ in / 62 cm, before felting

10 rnds in Plum

14 rnds in Dark Brown

10 rnds in Blackberry

14 rnds in Dark Brown

Bag Sides

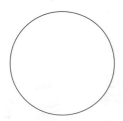

Bottom
Circumference: approx. 11 in / 28 cm, before felting

44 FELTED SHOULDER BAG

PATTERN

GAUGE
15 sts and 22 rows in St st = 4 x 4 in / 10 x 10 cm

PATTERN STITCHES
Stockinette Stitch (St st)
Flat: Knit on RS, purl on WS.
Circular: Knit all rnds.
Ribbing: (K1, p1) around.

INSTRUCTIONS
Lining
With Dark Brown and circular ndl, CO 120 sts. Join to work in the round, being careful not to twist.

Bag Sides
When piece measures approx. 24½ in / 62 cm, work stripes as shown on diagram, from top to bottom.
BO.

Bottom
Make a circle as follows:
With Blackberry, CO 8 sts and work back and forth in St st, and inc on RS rows as follows:
Inc Rnd 1: CO 4, work to end of row, turn, CO 4 at beg of next row.
Inc Rnds 2 and 3: CO 3, work to end of row, turn, CO 3 at beg of next row.
Inc Rnd 3: CO 2, work to end of row, turn, CO 2 at beg of next row.
Inc Rnds 5, 6, 7, 8, and 9: K1, m1, knit to last st, m1, k1.
You should now have 42 sts on the ndl. Work 18 rows without shaping. Then dec on RS rows as follows.
Dec Rnds 1, 2, 3, 4, and 5: K1, k2tog, knit to last 3 sts, ssk, k1.

Dec Rnd 6: BO 2, work to end of row, turn, BO 2 at beg of next row.
Dec Rnds 7 and 8: BO 3, work to end of row, turn BO 3 at beg of next row.
Dec Rnd 9: BO 4, work to end of row, turn, BO 4 at beg of next row.
You should now have 8 sts on the ndl. BO.

Strap
With Blackberry, CO 11 sts. Work in Ribbing for approx. 88 in / 225 cm. BO.

FINISHING

Fold the lining to the inside then sew the bottom onto the bag, joining the outer and inner layers.
Weave in ends.

Felt the pieces using hot water and the normal cycle in the washing machine. It may take up to 1 hour and 20 minutes to shrink to size. Felt the strap separately and sew it on after felting. The pieces should shrink by about ⅓. Allow the pieces to dry thoroughly.

Sew the strap onto the bag, attaching the ends of the straps onto the two sides of the bag with the middle of the strap forming the handle for the bag at the top. Sew both sides of each end of the strap to the sides of the bag.

The bag can be made at any size by casting on a different number of stitches. Just remember the pieces will shrink by about ⅓ during felting.

45 FELTED SHOPPING BAG

PATTERN

GAUGE
15 sts and 22 rows in St st = 4 x 4 in /
10 x 10 cm

PATTERN STITCHES
Stockinette Stitch (St st)
Flat: Knit on RS, purl on WS.
Circular: Knit all rnds.
Ribbing: (K1, p1) around.

INSTRUCTIONS
Lining
With Dark Brown and circular ndl, CO
140 sts. Join to work in the round,
being careful not to twist.

Bag Sides
When piece measures approx. 24½ in /
62 cm, work stripes as shown on
diagram, from top to bottom.
BO.

Bottom
Make a circle as follows:
With Blackberry, CO 16 sts and work
back and forth in St st, and inc on RS
rows as follows:
Inc Rnd 1: CO 5, work to end of row,
turn, CO 5 at beg of next row.
Inc Rnd 2: CO 4, work to end of row,
turn, CO 4 at beg of next row.
Inc Rnd 3: CO 3, work to end of row,
turn, CO 3 at beg of next row.
Inc Rnd 4: CO 2, work to end of row,
turn, CO 2 at beg of next row.
Inc Rnds 5, 6, 7, 8, and 9: K1, m1,
knit to last st, m1, k1.
You should now have 54 sts on the ndl.
Work 30 rows without shaping. Then
dec on RS rows as follows.
Dec Rnds 1, 2, 3, 4, and 5: K1, k2tog,
knit to last 3 sts, ssk, k1.

Dec Rnd 6: BO 2, work to end of row,
turn, BO 2 at beg of next row.
Dec Rnd 7: BO 3, work to end of row,
turn, BO 3 at beg of next row.
Dec Rnd 8: BO 4, work to end of row,
turn, BO 4 at beg of next row.
Dec Rnd 9: BO 5, work to end of row,
turn, BO 5 at beg of next row.
You should now have 16 sts on the ndl.
BO.

Handles (make 2)
With Dark Brown, CO 13 sts. Work in
Ribbing for approx. 16 in / 40 cm.
BO.

FINISHING

Fold the lining to the inside then sew
the bottom onto the bag, joining the
two layers.
Weave in ends.

Felt the pieces using hot water and the
normal cycle in the washing machine.
It may take up to 1 hour and 20
minutes to shrink to size. Felt the strap
separately and sew it on after felting.
The pieces should shrink by about ⅓.
Allow the pieces to dry thoroughly.

Sew the handles onto the two sides of
bag, with both ends of each handle
attached to the outside of the bag
several in (cm) apart. Stitch in place
around the overlapping portions.

The bag can be made at any size by
casting on a different number of
stitches. Just remember the pieces will
shrink by about ⅓ during felting.

MATERIALS

Yarn:
CYCA #4 (worsted/afghan/aran),
Landlust Tweed or equivalent
(87 yd/80 m / 50 g)

Yarn Amounts:
#4741 Dark Brown, 300 g
#4824 Grass Green, 150 g
#4885 Yellow Green, 50 g
#4805 Turquoise, 50 g

Knitting Needles:
U.S. size 10 / 6 mm circular
and straight needles

Finished Measurements:
Circumference: approx.
15 in / 38 cm, before felting

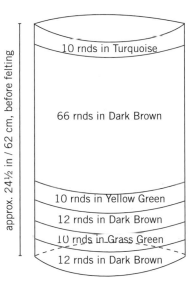

approx. 24½ in / 62 cm, before felting

10 rnds in Turquoise

66 rnds in Dark Brown

10 rnds in Yellow Green

12 rnds in Dark Brown

10 rnds in Grass Green

12 rnds in Dark Brown

Bag Sides

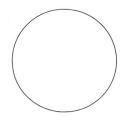

Bottom
Circumference: approx. 15 in / 38 cm,
before felting

MATERIALS

Yarn:
CYCA #4 (worsted/afghan/aran), Landlust Tweed or equivalent (87 yd/80 m / 50 g)

Yarn Amounts:
#4715 Dark Green, 100 g
#4898 Petrol Blue, 50 g
#4885 Yellow Green, 50 g

Knitting Needles:
U.S. size 8 / 5 mm

Notions:
Tapestry needle, approx. 32 in / 80 cm brown cotton cording, small pieces of orange and olive green wool felt, small orange button, small amounts of yarn in various colors for embroidery

Finished Measurements:
Finished size varies depending on gauge and felting

46 LITTLE COMPANION

PATTERN

GAUGE
17 sts and 15 rows in St st = 4 x 4 in / 10 x 10 cm

PATTERN STITCHES
Bag
Stockinette stitch (St st): Knit RS rows, purl WS rows.

Strap
Ribbing (over an odd number of sts): K1, p1 to last st, k1.

INSTRUCTIONS
For the bag, with Yellow Green, CO 44 sts. Work in St st for 40 rows. Change to Dark Green and work 150 rows in St st. BO.

220 rows Petrol Blue
(after felting, approx.
19¾ in / 50 cm)

Strap

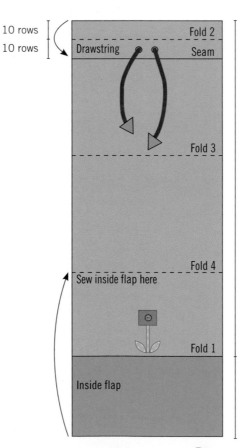

10 rows

10 rows

Drawstring

Fold 2

Seam

Fold 3

150 rows Dark Green
(after felting, approx.
22½ in / 57 cm)

Fold 4

Sew inside flap here

Fold 1

Inside flap

40 rows Yellow Green
(after felting, approx.
5 in / 13 cm)

Bag

For the strap, with Petrol Blue, CO 9 sts. Work in St st for 55 rows. Then work in ribbing for 110 rows, then work another 55 rows in St st. BO.

Following the diagram and using photo as a guide, for the flap lining, fold the bottom of the piece (the Yellow Green section) up at Line 1 with RS together and sew the side seams. Turn right side out and sew in place at Line 4.
For the drawstring pocket, fold the top of the piece down at Line 2 with RS together and sew in place, leaving the sides open.
For the bag body, fold the piece at Line 3 with RS facing. Overlap the ends of the straps with the sides of the bag and sew to the bag, letting the edges of the strap roll slightly. The strap ends become the sides of the bag.

Felt the pieces using hot water and the normal cycle in the washing machine. (With the water temperature at approx. 90°F / 30°C, the bag will felt only slightly. Use a higher temperature for a smaller, stronger bag.) Allow to dry thoroughly.

FINISHING

For the flower, cut stems and leaves from the olive green felt and the blossom from the orange felt. Use the embroidery yarn to sew the pieces onto the front of the bag, using the diagram and photo as a guide.
Beginning and ending at the center (as shown on the diagram), run the cord through the drawstring pocket, leaving approx. ½ in / 1 cm between the beginning and ending.
Cut 4 triangles from the olive green felt and sew 2 to each end of the cord to secure and cover the ends.

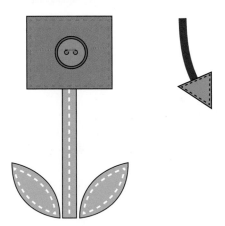

MATERIALS

Yarn:
CYCA #4 (worsted/afghan/
aran), Landlust Tweed or
equivalent (87 yd/80 m /
50 g)

Yarn Amounts:
#4741 Dark Brown, 650 g
#4843 Blackberry, 150 g
#4898 Petrol Blue, 150 g
#4847 Dark Turquoise, 150 g
#4805 Turquoise, 150 g
#4814 Plum, 100 g
#4816 Fuchsia, 50 g

Crochet Hook:
U.S. size 7 / 4.5 mm

Notions:
Tapestry needle, hairpin
lace loom

Finished Measurements:
Approx. 57 x 57 in / 145 x
145 cm

47 HAIRPIN LACE AFGHAN

PATTERN

INSTRUCTIONS
The afghan is made from 112 squares,
each measuring approx. 5 in / 13 cm.
The squares are sewn into strips first,
then the strips are sewn together.

Work each star at the center of each
square in Hairpin Lace as follows:

Set the width of the hairpin lace loom to
2 in / 5 cm. Attach yarn of the desired
color to the left prong of the loom with a
slip knot and make a strip of 32 x 2 loops
(1 loop of each pair is on the left prong
and the other is on the right prong). The
center of the strip is made with single
crochet stitches in the center of the work
after each rotation of the loom (see
drawings on page 117). Cut the yarn,
leaving a tail of approx. 4 in / 10 cm.

Cut a piece of yarn in the same color
approx. 6 in / 15 cm long. Draw this
through the 32 loops on the left prong of
the loom. Take the strip off the loom and
pull the two ends of this yarn together
and knot to form the center of the star.
Weave in the ends.

To finish the star, crochet around the
outside edge as follows:
Rnd 1: With Dark Brown, sc into the next
4 loops together. *Work 3 dc into the
next sc at the center of the strip before
the next loop, then work 1 sc into the
next 4 loops together;* rep from * to * 6
more times, work 3 dc into the next sc at
the center of the strip, and join with sl st
to first sc—a total 8 loops for the star
points. Turn.
Rnd 2: Ch 3, *2 dc into the same st, ch
3, sc in the center dc of the next group of
3 dc, ch 3, sc in the next sc, ch 3, sc in
the center dc of the next group of 3 dc,
ch 3, dc in the next sc;* rep from * to *
2 more times, 2 dc in the same st, ch 3,
sc in the center dc of the next group of 3
dc, ch 3, sc in the next sc, ch 3, sc in

ARRANGEMENT OF SQUARES

● Turquoise
□ Dark Turquoise
■ Petrol

△ Blackberry
▲ Plum
▣ Fuchsia

the center dc of the next group of 3 dc, ch 3 and dc in the 3rd ch from the beg of the rnd. Turn.

Rnd 3: Ch 3, *(sc in next ch sp, ch 3) twice, sc in next ch sp, ch 4, work next 3 sts together, dc in next 3 dc, ch 4; * sc in next ch sp; from * to * 3 more times, and join with slip st in next dc.

Make 112 squares in the following colors: 16 in Turquoise, 20 in Dark Turquoise, 28 in Petrol, 24 in Blackberry, 16 in Plum, and 8 in Fuchsia.

FINISHING

Crochet the 112 squares together with Dark Brown (see drawing, "Arrangement of Squares"). Place the individual squares RS together and join as follows: Work sc around the outer edge of the squares, inserting the hook into the next stitch of both pieces together. At the corners, work a dc through both pieces. After all the strips are completed, join them to form the blanket. Work a border around the afghan as follows: Join Dark Brown in a ch sp on the edge. Work around entire afghan with sc and ch spaces as follows:
On the sides: Ch 3 between each ch sp and sc in each ch sp.
On the outer corners: Ch 5 to go from one 4-ch sp to the next 4-ch sp.
On the inner corners (where 2 squares meet): Sc in last ch sp, ch 1, dc in corner st, ch 1, sc in first 4-ch sp of next square.

HAIRPIN LACE TECHNIQUE

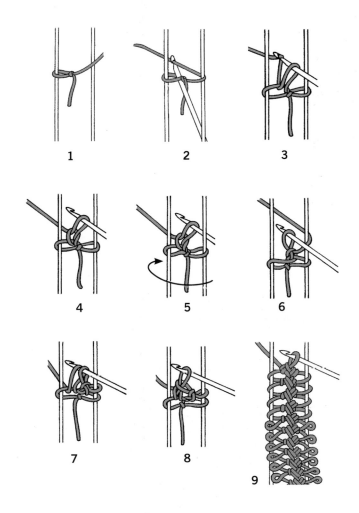

1

2

3

4

5

6

7

8

9

48/49 ROUND FLOOR CUSHIONS

SMALL CUSHION

MATERIALS

Yarn:
CYCA #4 (worsted/afghan/aran), Landlust Tweed or equivalent (87 yd/80 m / 50 g)

Yarn Amounts:
#5754 Landlust Red, 50 g
#4847 Dark Turquoise, 50 g
#2017 Light Gray, 50 g
#4741 Gray Brown, 50 g
#4596 Natural, 50 g

Knitting Needles:
U.S. size 8 or 9 / 5 or 5.5 mm

Notions:
Tapestry needle

Finished Measurements:
Approx. 20 in / 50 cm circumference

PATTERN

GAUGE
15 sts and 32 rows in garter stitch = 4 x 4 in / 10 x 10 cm

PATTERN STITCH
Garter Stitch: Knit all rows.

INSTRUCTIONS
With Landlust Red, CO 36 sts.
Row 1: K9, turn.
Row 2: Yo, k9 (to end of row).
Row 3: K9, knit the yo tog with the 10th st, k8, turn.
Row 4: Yo, k18 (to end of row).
Row 5: K18, knit the yo tog with the 19th st, k8, turn.
Row 6: Yo, k27 (to end of row).
Row 7: K27, knit the yo tog with the 28th st, k8, turn.
Row 8: K36.

Repeat Rows 1–8 for each wedge. With Landlust Red, work 1 more wedge, then work colors as follows:
4 wedges with Dark Turquoise
2 wedges in Light Gray
1 wedge in Dark Turquoise
1 wedge in Light Gray
2 wedges in Gray Brown
3 wedges in Landlust Red
2 wedges in Dark Turquoise
1 wedge in Light Gray
3 wedges in Natural
3 wedges in Gray Brown
2 wedges in Landlust Red
6 wedges in Light Gray
3 wedges in Natural
5 wedges in Gray Brown
6 wedges in Natural
1 wedge in Landlust Red
3 wedges in Gray Brown
1 wedge in Dark Turquoise
3 wedges in Light Gray
1 wedge in Natural
BO all sts.

FINISHING

Place the piece flat, forming a circle, and sew the CO and BO edges together. Weave in ends. For the bottom, cut a piece of fabric the size of the finished piece (plus 1 in / 2 cm for seam allowance). Sew to knitted piece, leaving a small opening. Fill cushion with stuffing and sew the opening closed. Sew button in the center of the cushion.

LARGE CUSHION

MATERIALS

Yarn:
CYCA #4 (worsted/afghan/aran), Landlust Tweed or equivalent (87 yd/80 m / 50 g)

Yarn Amounts:
#4814 Plum, 100 g
#2017 Light Gray, 100 g
#4741 Gray Brown, 100 g
#4596 Natural, 100 g
#4840 Orange, 50 g

Knitting Needles:
U.S. size 8 or 9 / 5 or 5.5 mm

Notions:
Tapestry needle

Finished Measurements:
Circumference: Approx. 20 in / 50 cm

GAUGE
15 sts and 32 rows in garter stitch = 4 x 4 in / 10 x 10 cm

PATTERN STITCH
Garter Stitch: Knit all rows.

50 EGG WARMERS

INSTRUCTIONS

With Orange, CO 50 sts.
Row 1: K20, turn.
Row 2: Yo, k20 (to end of row).
Row 3: K20, knit the yo tog with the 21st stitch, k9, turn.
Row 4: Yo, k30 (to end of row).
Row 5: K30, knit the yo tog with the 31st stitch, k9, turn.
Row 6: Yo, k40 (to end of row).
Row 7: K40, knit the yo tog with the 41st stitch, k9, turn.
Row 8: K50.
Rep Rows 1–8 for each wedge.
With Orange, work 1 more wedge, then work colors as follows:
4 wedges in Plum
2 wedges in Light Gray
1 wedge in Plum
1 wedge in Light Gray
2 wedges in Gray Brown
3 wedges in Orange
2 wedges in Plum
1 wedge in Light Gray
3 wedges in Natural
3 wedges in Gray Brown
2 wedges in Orange
6 wedges in Light Gray
2 wedges in Plum
3 wedges in Natural
5 wedges in Gray Brown
6 wedges in Natural
2 wedges in Orange
3 wedges in Gray Brown
1 wedge in Plum
3 wedges in Light Gray
5 wedges in Gray Brown
1 wedge in Plum
2 wedges in Natural
BO all sts.

FINISHING

See instructions for Large Cushion.

MATERIALS

Yarn:
CYCA #4 (worsted/afghan/aran), Landlust Tweed or equivalent (87 yd/80 m / 50 g)

Yarn Amounts:
Small amount of desired color

Crochet Hook:
U.S. size G-6 / 4 mm

Notions:
1 small button, sewing needle and matching thread

PATTERN

INSTRUCTIONS
For a Large Egg
Rnd 1: Ch 5 and join with a sl st to form a ring.
Rnd 2: Work 6 sc in ring, join with sl st, ch 1.
Rnd 3: Work 2 sc in each sc around, join with sl st, ch 1.
Rnd 4: (Sc in next sc, 2 sc in next sc) around, join with sl st, ch 1.
Rnd 5: Sc in each sc around, join with sl st, ch 1.
Rnd 6: (Sc in next 3 sc, 2 sc in next sc) around, join with sl st, ch 1.
Rnds 7 and 8: Sc in each sc around, join with sl st, ch 1.
Turn.
Rnd 9: Sc in each sc, stopping 2 sts before end of rnd, ch 1, turn.
Rnd 10: Sc in each sc, ch 1, turn.
Rnd 11: (Sc in next 7 sc, sk next sc) across.

FINISHING

With work on the left, at the end of Rnd 11, ch 12, sc to beg of rnd to form button loop. Sew on button with needle and thread.

MATERIALS

RED SEAT COVER

Yarn:
CYCA #4 (worsted/afghan/aran), Landlust Tweed or equivalent (87 yd/80 m / 50 g)

Yarn Amounts:
#4754 Landlust Red, 100 g

Crochet Hook:
U.S. size G-6 / 4 mm

Finished Measurements:
Approx. 14½ x 12 in / 37 x 30 cm

STRIPED SEAT COVER

Yarn:
CYCA #4 (worsted/afghan/aran), Landlust Tweed or equivalent (87 yd/80 m / 50 g)

Yarn Amounts:
#4754 Landlust Red, 20 g
#4816 Fuchsia, 20 g
#4847 Dark Turquoise, 20 g
#4824 Grass Green, 20 g
#4840 Orange, 20 g

Crochet Hook:
U.S. size G-6 / 4 mm

Notions:
Approx. 16 in / 40 cm of elastic

Finished Measurements:
Approx. 12 x 11 in / 30 x 28 cm

51/52 BICYCLE SEAT COVERS

RED SEAT COVER

GAUGE
14 hdc and 11 rows = 4 x 4 in / 10 x 10 cm

PATTERN STITCHES
Chain
Half Double Crochet

INSTRUCTIONS
Ch 25.
Row 1: Hdc in 2nd st from hook and next 21 ch, 2 hdc in last ch.
Rows 2–9: Ch 2 (counts as 1 hdc), hdc in each hdc across, 2 hdc in last hdc (39 sts).
Rows 10–15: Ch 2 (counts as 1 hdc), hdc across.
Rows 16–18: 2 hdc tog, hdc across to last 2 sts, 2 hdc tog (33 sts).
Rows 19–20: 3 hdc tog, hdc across to last 3 sts, 3 hdc tog (25 sts).
Rows 21–22: 2 hdc tog, hdc across to last 2 sts, 2 hdc tog (21 sts).
Row 23: Ch 2 (counts as 1 hdc), hdc across.

Row 24: 2 hdc tog, hdc across to last 2 sts, 2 hdc tog (19 sts).
Rows 25–57: Ch 2 (counts as 1 hdc), hdc across.
Row 28: 2 hdc tog, hdc across to last 2 sts, 2 hdc tog (17 sts).
Row 29: Ch 2 (counts as 1 hdc), hdc across.
Rows 30–33: 2 hdc tog, hdc across to last 2 sts, 2 hdc tog (9 sts).
Rows 34–35: Ch 2 (counts as 1 hdc), hdc across.
Fasten off.

Work in rounds as follows:
Rnd 1: Join with sl st in middle of first row. Ch 2, then work around edge in hdc (about 110 sts, total must be divisible by 10).
Rnds 2–4: Hdc around.
Rnd 5: Ch 5, *sk 2 hdc, dc in next hdc, ch 1, sk 1, dc in next hdc, ch 2 dd;* rep from * to * around and then end with 1 dc.

FINISHING

Weave in ends. Make a chain approx 39 in / 100 cm long. Weave this chain through the holes on the last rnd and tie ends to fasten the seat cover onto the seat.

STRIPPED SEAT COVER

GAUGE
14 hdc and 11 rows = 4 x 4 in / 10 x 10 cm

PATTERN STITCHES
See chart.

INSTRUCTIONS
With desired color, ch 28. Work Rows 1-29 as follows or following chart.

Row 1: Dc in 19th ch (counting from beg of ch), ch 2, *dc in next 3 ch, ch 2;* rep from * to * across, end with 1 dc.

Row 2: Ch 3 (counts as 1 dc), dc in ch from prev row, *ch 2, 3 dc in next ch sp;* rep from * to * across (7 clusters). Change colors.

Row 3: Ch 5, *3 dc in ch from prev row, ch 2;* rep from * to * across (6 clusters).

Rows 4–7: Rep Rows 2 and 3.

Row 8: Ch 5, 3 dc in ch from prev row, *ch 2, 3 dc in next ch sp;* rep from * to * across (7 clusters).

Row 9: Ch 3 (counts as 1 dc), 2 dc in last st of prev row, *ch 2, 3 dc in next ch sp;* rep from * to * across (8 clusters). Change colors.

Row 10: Ch 1 (counts as 1 dc), 2 dc in last st of prev row, *ch 2, 3 dc in next ch sp;* rep from * to * across and work the last cluster in the last st of the prev row (9 clusters). Change colors.

Row 11: Rep Row 10 (10 clusters).

Row 12: Rep Row 10 (11 clusters).

Row 13: Ch 5, *3 dc in ch sp of prev row, ch 2; * rep from * to *, ending with 1 dc (10 clusters). Change colors.

Row 14: Ch 3 (counts as 1 dc), 2 dc in ch sp of prev row, *ch 2, 3 dc in next ch sp; * rep from * to * across (11 clusters). Change colors.

Rows 15 and 16: Rep Rows 13 and 14.

Row 17: Rep Row 10 (12 clusters).

Row 18: Rep Row 13 (12 clusters).

Row 19: Rep Row 17 (12 clusters).

Row 20: Rep Row 10 (13 clusters).

Row 21: Rep Row 13 (12 clusters).

Row 22: Ch 3 (counts as 1 dc), 2 dc in first dc of prev row; *ch 2, 3 dc in next ch sp;* rep from * to * across, ending with 1 dc in last ch sp of prev row (12 clusters). Change colors.

Row 23: Ch 3 (counts as 1 dc), * 3 dc in next ch sp, ch 2; * rep from * to * across, end with 1 dc in last ch sp of prev row (11 clusters). Change colors.

Row 24: Rep Row 23 (10 clusters).

Row 25: Rep Row 10 (9 clusters).

Row 26: Rep Row 10 (8 clusters).

Row 27: Rep Row 10 (7 clusters).

Row 28: Rep Row 10 (6 clusters).

Row 29: Rep Row 10 (5 clusters).

Change colors and begin working in the round around the outside edge of the piece. Ch 3, *2 dc in next ch sp, ch 1, dc in next cluster;* rep from * to * around and on the corners work 3 dc in the ch sp. Join with sl st and fasten off.

FINISHING
Weave in ends. Run the elastic through the edges of the seat cover and gather in to fit on seat. Tie ends together.

CHART KEY

○ ch

† dc

⤬| 2 dc in same st

⤬| 3 dc in same st

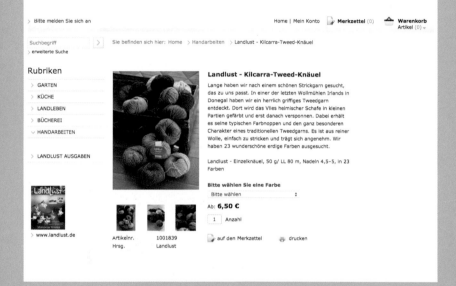

Yarn Information

For years, the *Landlust* editors have been working with talented designers to create beautiful knitting and crochet patterns with Landlust Kilcarra Tweed yarn. These patterns, kits, and yarns are listed on their website (shop.landlust.de/landlust-tweed-knauel.html). A color chart for reference is on the following two pages.

American knitters unable to obtain any of the yarn used in this book can substitute yarn of a similar weight and composition. Please note, however, the finished projects may vary slightly from those shown, depending on the yarn used. Donegal Luxury Tweed Aran from Debbie Bliss and Donegal Tweed from Tahki are widely available alternatives; or try www.yarnsub.com for other suggestions.

Webs – America's Yarn Store
75 Service Center Road
Northampton, MA 01060
800-367-9327
www.yarn.com
customerservice@yarn.com

LoveKnitting.com
www.loveknitting.com/us

For more information on selecting or substituting yarn, contact your local yarn shop or an online store; they are familiar with all types of yarns and would be happy to help you. Additionally, the online knitting community at Ravelry.com has forums where you can post questions about specific yarns. Yarns come and go so quickly these days and there are so many beautiful yarns available.

2017 * Light Gray 1857 *	4742 Medium Gray 1877	4582 Stone Gray 1840	4581 Dark Gray 1858	4741 Dark Brown 1856

Landlust -Tweed

4756 Green 1843	4715 Dark Green 1879	4898 Petrol 1839	4847 Dark Turquoise 1919	4843 Blackberry 1841

4817	4596	4805	4728	4885	4824
Gray Brown	Natural	Turquoise	Yellow	Yellow Green	Grass Green
1909	1878	1876	1949	1859	1918

100% virgin wool
87 yd/80 m / 50 g per skein
A women's sweater takes approx. 600 g

4 x 4 in /
10 x 10 cm

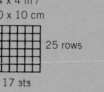

25 rows

17 sts

U.S. size 7-8 /
4.5-5 mm ndls

4814	4816	4854	4802	4840	4754
Plum	Fuchsia	Rose	Rust	Orange	Landlust Red
1916	1917	1948	1842	1920	1896

GAUGE SWATCH

Before you begin a project you should make a swatch using the suggested size needles. Cast on enough stitches to work a swatch that is at least 4 x 4 in / 10 x 10 cm in the pattern stitch specified. Count the number of stitches and rows in 4 in / 10 cm. If you have more stitches than recommended, try again with a larger needle. If you have fewer stitches than recommended, try again with a smaller needle.

GAUGE 4 X 4 IN / 10 X 10 CM